BACKROADS

—— *of* ——

OREGON

BACKROADS

—— *of* ——

OREGON

Your Guide to Oregon's Most Scenic
Backroad Adventures

Text by Rhonda Ostertag
Photography by George Ostertag

Voyageur Press

Discovery A Pictorial Guide

Edited by Amy Rost and Kari Cornell
Designed by Andrea Rud
Printed in China

05   06   07   08   09   5   4   3   2   1

Library of Congress Cataloging-in-Publication Data

Ostertag, Rhonda, 1957-
   Backroads of Oregon : your guide to Oregon's most scenic backroad adventures / text by Rhonda Ostertag ; photography by George Ostertag.
      p. cm. — (A pictorial discovery guide)
   Includes bibliographical references and index.
   ISBN 0-89658-081-4 (pbk. : alk. paper)
   1. Scenic byways—Oregon—Guidebooks. 2. Automobile travel—Oregon—Guidebooks. 3. Oregon—Tours. 4. Oregon—Pictorial works. I. Ostertag, George, 1957- II. Title. III. Series.
   F874.3.O85 2004
   917.95004′44′091734—dc22
                           2004024717

Published by Voyageur Press, Inc.
123 North Second Street, P.O. Box 338, Stillwater, MN 55082 U.S.A.
651-430-2210, fax 651-430-2211
books@voyageurpress.com
www.voyageurpress.com

Educators, fundraisers, premium and gift buyers, publicists, and marketing managers: Looking for creative products and new sales ideas? Voyageur Press books are available at special discounts when purchased in quantities, and special editions can be created to your specifications. For details contact the marketing department at 800-888-9653.

FRONT COVER:
Rowena Loops on Historic Columbia River Highway

TITLE PAGE, MAIN PHOTO:
At a depth of 1,958 feet, Crater Lake is the second deepest natural lake in the Western Hemisphere and the seventh deepest in the world. Crater Lake National Park is Oregon's only national park.

TITLE PAGE, INSET:
Columbia lilies decorate the meadows and forests of the Oregon Cascades.

CONTENTS

INTRODUCTION 7

PART I THE NORTHWEST: STERLING COAST TO VERDANT VALLEY 11
Northwest Passage: Nehalem Highway to Historic Astoria and Fort Clatsop 12
Capes Crusade: Three Capes Scenic Route and Nestucca River National Back Country Byway 17
Land of Falling Waters: Silver Falls Tour Route 21
All Things Coastal: Pacific Coast Scenic Byway, Central Section 25
Heart of the Valley: Benton County Scenic Loop 32
Spans across Time: Covered Bridge Country Tour 36

PART II THE NORTHERN CASCADES: VOLCANOES, FORESTS, AND WILD AND SCENIC WATERS 39
Hail Columbia!: Historic Columbia River Highway 40
Rounding Wy'East: Mount Hood–Lost Lake Loop 45
On the Western Slope: West Cascades Scenic Byway, Clackamas-Breitenbush Section 49
It All Begins at Home, Sweet Home: Quartzville National Back Country Byway 53
Volcano Central: McKenzie Pass–Santiam Pass Scenic Byway 56
Into the Forest: Robert Aufderheide Memorial Drive 60
On the Eastern Slope: Cascade Lakes Scenic Byway 64

PART III THE SOUTHWEST: JEFFERSON COUNTRY 67
Driving Rivers: Rogue-Umpqua Scenic Byway 72
Siskiyous to the Sea: Rogue-Coquille Scenic Byway 76
Fire and Feathers: Volcanic Legacy Scenic Byway 81
Rogue Journey: Galice-Hellgate and Grave Creek to Marial National Back Country Byways 88

PART IV THE NORTHEAST: COLUMBIA PLATEAU TO WALLOWA HIGH COUNTRY 91
Chutes and Fly-lines: Lower Deschutes River National Back Country Byway 96
John Day Country: Journey Through Time Scenic Byway 100
Singing the Blues: Blue Mountain Scenic Byway 105
Paradise Found: Hells Canyon Scenic Byway, Main Loop 109
Ghosts of Gold: Elkhorn Scenic Byway 113
Going Crooked: Lower Crooked River National Back Country Byway 120
The Road Less Traveled: Paulina/Izee Highway 121

PART V THE SOUTHEAST: OREGON OUTBACK 127
Roam on the Range: Oregon Outback Scenic Byway 128
Desert Tidings: Christmas Valley National Back Country Byway 133
Pioneers and Palisades: Leslie Gulch–Succor Creek Backroad 137
Cowboys, Cranes, and Craters: Malheur National Wildlife Refuge–Diamond Loop 141
Out of the Desert: Steens Mountain National Back Country Byway 148
Where the Antelope Play: Lakeview to Steens Mountain National Back Country Byway 152

INDEX 156
SUGGESTED RESOURCES 159
ABOUT THE AUTHOR AND PHOTOGRAPHER 160

INTRODUCTION

We feel lucky to live in Oregon and to have this chance to honor her splendor in photographs and words. Over the past twenty years, we've criss-crossed the state hundreds of times, both to research our previous outdoor Oregon guidebooks and just for fun. We feel we know the state and her roads pretty well. Oregon is much more than a place or even a state of mind—Oregon is the promise of something grand over the horizon, the western dream. That promise beckoned our earliest pioneers and still dwells in the hearts and minds of Oregonians today. By exploring the state, travelers come to appreciate the character of her people.

Oregon rolls out visual diversity with stunning landscapes of coast, mountain, valley, canyon, lava plain, and desert. Her routes introduce senses of the bucolic, the rugged, the delicate, and even the bizarre. Indeed, Oregon has a wealth of accessible routes that do justice to the state's many treasures. For us, it was a case of narrowing the list. Some routes may wear the numbers of primary highways, but the surrounding lonesome outback gives them backroads appeal.

We've included many federal-, state-, and county-designated drives. While U.S. Bureau of Land Management (BLM) backroads have the label "National Back Country Byways," many U.S. Forest Service (USFS) routes have been incorporated into the state's scenic byway system. Presently, Oregon has nine national routes recognized by Congress. Four of the routes hold the highest distinction, "All-American": the Pacific Coast Highway,

FACING PAGE:

Upper Proxy Falls in the Three Sisters Wilderness nurtures a lush gallery of moss and greenery. The porous lava at its base swallows the creek, giving the impression of a bottomless pool.

ABOVE:

The classic 120-foot span of Gilkey Covered Bridge was built in 1939 and underwent reconditioning in 1998. Its mostly open sides overlook Thomas Creek.

the Historic Columbia River Highway, the Volcanic Legacy Scenic Byway, and the Hells Canyon Scenic Byway.

For the most part, routes are paved and suitable for passenger vehicles. However, several drives have improved gravel sections, and the Steens Mountain byway is all gravel. Generally, the offerings more than compensate for the bounce and dust. On some roads, travelers may go great distances without spying another vehicle. On a handful of other roads, commuter or through traffic will hurry travelers along, but these routes have winning attractions and offer frequent stops for relaxation.

Suggested stops include parks, wildlife areas, geologic wonders, picnic spots, trails, fishing holes, vistas, ghost towns, museums, "U-pick" farms, general stores, festivals, and more. Many stunning rivers, lakes, and waterfalls grace the state thanks to her notorious rains. Travelers will cross swords with history, encountering the likes of Chief Comcomly (on the northern coast), Chief Joseph (in northeast Oregon), Lewis and Clark, John C. Fremont, and hearty pioneers. Wildlife—bald eagles, sandhill cranes, coyotes, deer, and antelope—make for unexpected stops.

Among the selected routes is the highest-climbing road in Oregon, the Steens Mountain byway, which tops 9,700 feet. Like a few other routes, it has a brief travel window (July through October), but it's worth the effort to see. Seasonal changes can rewrite the story of a drive.

Some routes seem to carry travelers across time as well as place. For city dwellers, backroads offer a pleasant change of pace—fellow travelers wave hello instead of gesturing in anger.

In this fast-paced world, the art of leisurely touring may take some practice. It's not about making time, getting somewhere, or miles per hour, but about the going. It's about giving in to curiosity. What's around the next bend, down that side road, or behind that curio shop door? Instead of golden arches and Whoppers, it's about cozy diners, blue-plate specials, and personally tasting "the world's best blackberry pie."

Binoculars and cameras should be at the ready. While most trips can be logistically accomplished in a matter of hours, giving in to their spell can stretch even the shortest drives into a day or a week. Bed and breakfasts, campgrounds, historic hotels, and family-operated motels may suggest an overnight or extended stay.

For backroad travel, especially in remote reaches where traffic is light and towns are distant and small, motorists need to take steps to ensure safe travel. The most important step is to start with a vehicle and tires in good repair and a full gas tank, to be topped-off whenever possible. A cell phone is a good traveler's aid but is not fail proof; reception may be spotty in isolated areas. An easy safeguard is to let family or friends know of travel plans and to advise them of any changes.

Maps are invaluable for staying on course, but also for suggesting side trips, shortcuts, or bypasses, should the situation require it. Most of the national and state designated scenic byways have signs or brochures (sometimes both) to help keep readers on course. Brochures with information on these drives are often available at welcome centers and chambers of commerce along the routes. For BLM or USFS routes, agency offices provide information. The Oregon Tourism Commission can help readers gather additional travel information.

Some parking areas and recreation sites on federal lands require either a daily fee/pass or an annual universal pass to federal lands. The universal passes provide access to national parks, forests, and wildlife refuges, as well as Bureau of Land Management and Corps of Engineering sites. State parks have their own daily and annual pass system.

The selected drives in this book only tap the surface of what's out there, but they provide a good representation of Oregon, her many merits, and the adventure of the backroad. Whatever you seek—the pounding surf, the moist breath of a waterfall, an open sagebrush expanse, a rip-roaring rodeo, or a dusty corner in an old museum—it is out there waiting for you in Oregon.

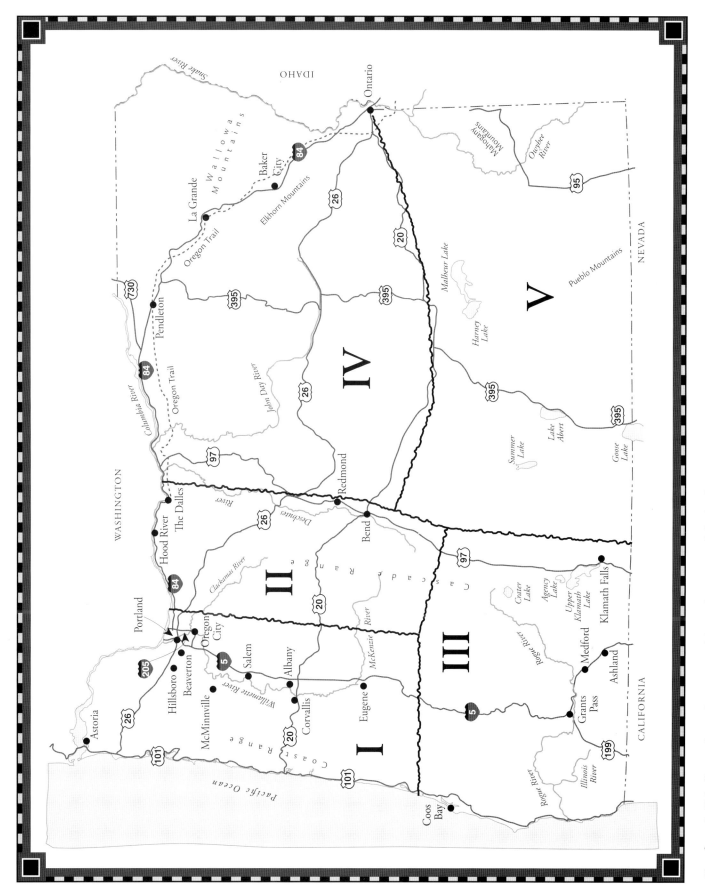

Numbers I–V indicate the regions covered in each section of the book.

PART I

THE NORTHWEST: STERLING COAST TO VERDANT VALLEY

FACING PAGE:

Rugged, forested headlands plunge to the ocean, punctuating the Oregon Coast. This is the northern view from Strawberry Hill Picnic Area, where fog often clings to the coast.

ABOVE:

Oregon's Willamette Valley is noted for its berries. Ice cream makers and jam and jelly companies favor the flavor-intense berries. At U-pick farms and produce stands, travelers can sample the bounty.

A spectacular coast, the forgotten Coast Range Mountains, and the Eden of the Willamette Valley all compose the northwest of Oregon. It's no wonder that settlement occurred here. This region now holds the state's primary population centers. Because of its popularity and its population, some routes can be busy. Nonetheless, the natural assets win out.

The coast boasts long, unbroken sandy strands, as well as rocky coves, headlands, and sea stacks. Decorating the shore are wind-sculpted dunes; ports and tourist towns; and forests of old-growth and second-growth Sitka spruce, shore pine, Douglas fir, and western hemlock. The coastal lowlands support dairy cows. The northern coast is a place of cloaking fog, incredible sunbursts, and invigorating salt breezes—a place of romance, lighthouses, ghosts, and shipwrecks.

Rising to the east, the steep-sided peaks of the coastal mountains rake rain from the clouds and wear the cloak of a temperate rainforest. The mountains suggest the characters of Indian legend and serve as landmarks for modern-day explorers as they did for the first explorers. Prized rivers, wildlife, waterfalls, and trees of record-setting height, girth, and age are just part of the attraction. Trails provide a more intimate look at these splendors. The history of logging can be seen in the mottled tapestry of the landscape. Although not as plentiful as in the past, salmon and steelhead still struggle up the waterways.

East of the mountains stretches the promised land of the Willamette Valley, made for a lazy summer afternoon. In the mid 1800s, Oregon Trail pioneers braved two thousand miles of hardship to reach this fertile land. The broad Willamette River, born in the Cascades, wends its way north through the valley to meet the mighty Columbia River in Portland. The rich valley soils that produce a smorgasbord of crops and the sumptuous tastes of summer arrived in the turbulent Missoula Floods at the end of the last ice age.

Logging, farming, and fishing continue to hold a place in the region's economy, bumping shoulders with high-tech industries and tourism. Oregon has a strong environmental voice. Although citizens in this region and throughout the state can express vastly different political and economic opinions from one another, an emotional tie to the land unites them.

NORTHWEST PASSAGE
Nehalem Highway to Historic Astoria and Fort Clatsop

ROUTE 1

From U.S. Highway 26 west of Portland, Nehalem Highway heads north on Oregon Highway 47 and west on Highway 202 from Mist to Astoria. From Astoria, Fort Clatsop sits to the southwest; marked routes to the fort follow U.S. 101 or U.S. 101 Business.

This 80-mile serpentine arc travels across Oregon's lightly inhabited northwest corner through coastal mountain forests and rural valleys. Astoria, at journey's end, housed the first settlement west of the Rockies. Its history begins with the coastal Indians, who helped Meriwether Lewis and William Clark and later the settlers of John Jacob Astor's Pacific Fur Company. After the waning of the fur-trade era, the towering western red cedars, Douglas firs, and Sitka spruce pushed logging to the forefront of this region's economy, and it remains a mainstay today. Located where the

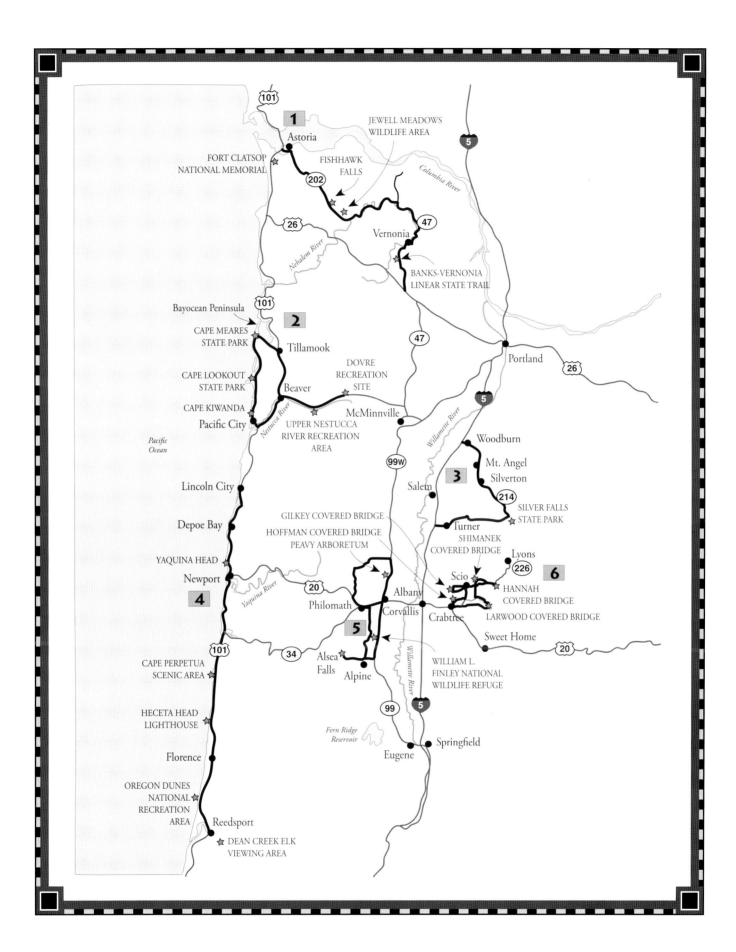

101

1

Astoria

JEWELL MEADOWS
WILDLIFE AREA

FORT CLATSOP
NATIONAL MEMORIAL

FISHHAWK
FALLS

202

Columbia River

5

26

Vernonia

47

Nehalem River

BANKS-VERNONIA
LINEAR STATE TRAIL

47

Bayocean Peninsula

101

2

Portland

26

CAPE MEARES
STATE PARK

Tillamook

DOVRE
RECREATION
SITE

5

CAPE LOOKOUT
STATE PARK

Beaver

Woodburn

Mt. Angel

Silverton

CAPE KIWANDA

McMinnville

3

Pacific City

Nestucca River

UPPER NESTUCCA
RIVER RECREATION
AREA

99W

Salem

214

SILVER FALLS
STATE PARK

Pacific
Ocean

Willamette River

Lincoln City

GILKEY COVERED BRIDGE

Turner

SHIMANEK
COVERED BRIDGE

Depoe Bay

HOFFMAN COVERED BRIDGE
PEAVY ARBORETUM

Lyons

226

6

YAQUINA HEAD

Scio

HANNAH
COVERED BRIDGE

Newport

Yaquina River

20

Albany

4

Philomath

Corvallis

Crabtree

LARWOOD COVERED BRIDGE

5

Sweet Home

101

34

Alsea
Falls

Alpine

Willamette River

WILLIAM L.
FINLEY NATIONAL
WILDLIFE REFUGE

20

CAPE PERPETUA
SCENIC AREA

HECETA HEAD
LIGHTHOUSE

99

5

Florence

Fern Ridge
Reservoir

Eugene

Springfield

OREGON DUNES
NATIONAL
RECREATION
AREA

Reedsport

DEAN CREEK ELK
VIEWING AREA

Fishhawk Creek and Lee Wooden County Park offer a quiet roadside retreat near Jewell Meadows. This Coast Range creek receives steady winter rain and has a temperate rainforest environment.

BELOW:

At the entry to Astoria, travelers are greeted by the lined face of "Whispering Giant," a cedar woodcarving by Peter Wolf Toth. The carving represents the Clatsop, Chinook, and all Northwest Coastal Indians.

RIGHT:

Roosevelt elk browse the rich grasses of Jewell Meadows Wildlife Area. The elk linger throughout the year, but are most visible from fall through spring. In winter, visitors can make arrangements to participate in the feeding of the elk.

Misnamed after the daughter of an early settler, Vernonia is representative of the historic small logging towns dotting the Coast Range. The town, which marks the northern terminus of the Banks-Vernonia State Trail, has a "Main Street" with yesteryear charm.

BELOW:

The waterfront of Astoria once bustled with fishing boats and canneries, winning it the nickname, "the salmon-canning capital of the world." Today's waterfront attractions include a trolley, marinas, Fisherman's Memorial, the Columbia River Maritime Museum, barking sea lions, and the Queen of the West *sternwheeler.*

Columbia River meets the Pacific Ocean, Astoria's enterprises grew to include shipping, fishing, and canning. In the coastal forest southwest of Astoria, Fort Clatsop National Memorial holds the replica fort of Lewis and Clark's Corps of Discovery.

The Nehalem Highway pursues the Nehalem River, Fishhawk Creek, Klaskanine River, and the Youngs River tidal bay. Elk, country museums, cottage enterprises, a fish hatchery, and general stores number among the sights and stops. Nearly from the start, Oregon Highway 47 provides access to Banks-Vernonia Linear State Trail, the state's first rail trail, stretching nearly 21 miles. Some of the original wooden trestles still span the country highway. Open to hiking and cycling, this trail offers a slower appreciation of the river valley and woods. An unbroken 14-mile stretch heads south from Vernonia's riverside Anderson Park.

Tiny Vernonia greets visitors with its clean-scrubbed "Main Street" appeal, including sidewalks adorned in flags, flower boxes, and old-fashioned street lamps. Shop windows urge visitors to cup their eyes for a closer look. Discovery can include a frozen-in-time barbershop worthy of "Floyd the Barber" from television's fictional town of Mayberry.

Rolling across the coastal mountains, Highway 202's windshield views flip-flop between country and forest scenes. At Jewell Meadows Wildlife Area, formal turnouts allow for the safe viewing and photographing of elk. At the winter feeding site, a kiosk provides information about the elk and their habitats. Public restrooms at the site serve travelers.

Sometimes the elk are out in number; other times they remain secreted in the adjoining forest. Mornings and evenings are the best times for viewing elk. Seasonal changes such as ruts and calving can alter a herd's mix and behavior. After spring showers, the bulky beasts can shake a whole cloud's worth of rain from their fur. Autumn days echo with the clash of massive antlers. Deer, turkeys, hawks, and songbirds can fill binocular viewfinders at any time.

Past Jewell Meadows, an easily missed turn descends left into Lee Wooden (Clatsop County) Park, where Fishhawk Falls spills 100 feet, angling and skipping over the broken cliff.

On arrival at Astoria, signs and painted tower-emblems on the road mark the route to the Astoria Column atop Coxcomb Hill, the high ridge between the Columbia River and Youngs Bay. The column stands 125 feet high. Its exterior is painted in a sepia-like scroll of the region's history that spirals up the tower from the base to the balcony. Tracing the legend skyward, eyes brush upon the names of Robert Gray, John Jacob Astor, and Lewis and Clark. Inside, a climb up 164 stairs leads to the column balcony and clear-day views of the ocean, Coast Range, Astoria, the Columbia and Youngs rivers and their bridges, and even Washington's Mount Saint Helens and Mount Rainier. Sharing the hilltop is the burial-canoe memorial to Chinook Chief Comcomly, who befriended Lewis and Clark and helped the Astorians build Fort Astoria in 1811. From the summit of

Coxcomb Hill, a 1.5-mile trail descends to Cathedral Tree, an ancient spruce taller than the column.

Astoria's waterfront—with its fishermen's memorial, barking sea lions, cruise liners, and acclaimed Columbia River Maritime Museum—stirs the salt in one's blood, while the town's graceful Victorian houses and museums feed memories of days gone by. More than forty town buildings are on the National Register of Historic Places. The Riverfront Trolley, a restored 1913 streetcar, offers a convenient cross-town mode of travel; views from the trolley reveal the once-bustling waterfront, now in ruin or undergoing revitalization.

Fort Clatsop National Memorial puts a moving signature on the end of the tour. Here, Lewis and Clark and the Corps of Discovery braved a long Pacific Coast winter of relentless rain, spoiled meat, and an uncertain return east. In the fort's dark, cramped, spartan quarters, the explorers passed their time updating journals, making candles, tanning hides, and sewing moccasins.

Museum exhibits, journal entries, and living history demonstrations (during the summer months) bring the story together. A copy of the simple posting left behind by the departing corps is displayed at the fort. It lists the corps members, announces the completion of their mission, and asks that whoever reads it make the corps' accomplishment known to the "civilized world." Other copies of this notice were distributed to area natives, and one made it to Philadelphia via China in 1807. With the bicentennial celebration of the Lewis and Clark expedition, the civilized world is re-acknowledging that feat.

Note: An NPS shuttle is the only way to access the park during the summers of 2004 through 2006, while the park is celebrating the expedition's bicentennial. Call the NPS reservation line, listed in the "Suggested Resources" section, for reservations.

CAPES CRUSADE
Three Capes Scenic Route and
Nestucca River National Back Country Byway

This road trip out of Tillamook unites the wonder of the coast, the relaxation of the valley, and a state scenic waterway of the Coast Range. Hearty smells tweak the nostrils: the briny breeze, the recent catch, sweet grass, and dairy cows. More than 150 working dairy farms give the valley a patchwork appearance and supply milk for the town's signature Tillamook Cheese. Tillamook's easy country pace sets it apart from other coastal towns. Weaving the spell are the cheese factories, Pioneer Museum, and Latimer Quilt Museum. In August, the atmosphere is enhanced by the county fair, noted for its hilarious Pig 'N' Ford Races, which unite Model-Ts and protesting pigs. A train excursion or visit to the Blimp Air Museum is a good way to cap a visit to the town.

ROUTE 2

From U.S. Highway 101 in the Tillamook city center, follow the well-marked Three Capes Scenic Route west for a counterclockwise tour, looping back via U.S. 101. At Beaver, on U.S. 101, the trip's byway spur pursues Nestucca River Road 25 miles into the Upper Nestucca River Recreation Area, turning around at Dovre Recreation Site. The total trip is 112 miles.

RIGHT:

Tillamook is noted for its fine cheese, and the Blue Heron French Cheese Company is one of two cheese factories that welcomes the public. The rivers feeding into Tillamook Bay have shaped a flat, verdant farmland that is ideally suited for dairy herds.

BELOW:

The rich grasses of Tillamook County nourish dairy cows, whose milk is used to produce top-quality cheeses and other dairy products.

ABOVE:

Sitka spruces punctuate this offshore view from Cape Meares. In spring and fall, gray whales migrate along the Oregon coast, adding to the excitement of ocean viewing.

LEFT:

This mossy bigleaf maple drapes out over the Nestucca River State Scenic Waterway. The river travels 55 miles through the Coast Range and supports both Chinook salmon and steelhead.

Jam-packed with beauty and equal parts excitement and relaxation, Three Capes Scenic Route knits together capes and bays, superb ocean beaches, dramatic headlands, sand dunes, and vistas of a string of rock islands where seabirds nest. Trails at the parks along the route lead to more special vistas and settings. Beachcombing, sunset gazing, crabbing, clamming, and hang gliding are just a few of the activities visitors can enjoy during the road trip.

The capes route crosses the Trask River, passing through dairy flatlands before swinging north toward Bayocean Peninsula and trading farm scenes for Tillamook Bay impressions. For many, the peninsula is the first stop along the route. In the early 1900s, Bayocean was a bustling resort with family bungalows, paved streets, a natatorium, and an elegant hotel. But by midcentury, the sea had licked up any trace of town. Today, a natural jut welcomes visitors with its 3.5 miles of ocean beach and bay shore, both ideal for strolling. Walkers sometimes share the beach with horseback riders and the bay path with bicyclists. Visitors train binoculars on ospreys, bald eagles, herons, loons, and surf scoters.

Twisting along the coast, the route stitches together the trio of prized capes and their respective state parks: Cape Meares, Cape Lookout, and Cape Kiwanda. Cape Meares State Park (day use only) features a descriptively named octopus tree and an appealing mantle of Sitka spruce. An 1890 lighthouse, the shortest in Oregon at 38 feet tall, sits atop a 200-foot-high cliff. It looks out over the water to Three Arch Rocks, the first national wildlife refuge west of the Mississippi. The refuge supports Oregon's largest breeding colony of tufted puffins. Peregrine falcons actively nest on the cape's cliffs.

Jutting into Netarts Bay is Cape Lookout State Park. Available for both day use and for camping, this park offers a lightly traveled 5-mile sand spit, sunset cliffs, and a dramatic headland traversed by a trail. Harbor seals haul out on the tip of the spit. The headland overlooks wave-assaulted cliffs and is a good place from which to spot gray whales. During their spring migration north from Mexico, nearly 20,000 gray whales will travel the ocean along the Oregon coastline. They are concentrated in a 2-mile-wide band within viewing distance of shore. A remarkable average of ten whales per hour will pass this headland.

The drive forgoes the turnoff to Sand Lake Off-road Vehicle Area and instead edges the pastures and marsh of the Sand Lake estuary en route to Pacific City. Born a fishing village, Pacific City is home to Cape Kiwanda State Park and gateway to Bob Straub State Park at Nestucca Spit. Cape Kiwanda wins-over visitors with its dunes, golden sandstone cliffs, photogenic Haystack Rock, hang gliders, and its Dory Festival in July. Dories are flat-bottomed fishing boats launched directly into the teeth of the surf. In the fleet's heyday, 300 dories a day might launch from the beach. With the decline in salmon populations, the dories today take to the water for tradition rather than for profit making.

On the U.S. 101 return to Tillamook, the tiny communities of Cloverdale, Hebo, and Beaver (the start for the river-road trip) tick off distance. Scenery can include the Nestucca River, farm stands, and more black-and-white bovines. Elk and deer sometimes visit the dairy pastures.

The crooked Nestucca River byway enjoys a rural backdrop as it criss-crosses the river. Mossy maples, red alders, and conifers shade both slope and stream. The river is a pleasing sight with its bends, straightaways, and mossy rock bed. Although the canyon hillsides wear the mosaic of timberland, a tranquil bower of leaves and boughs often envelops the drive. Classic-car rallies sometimes use this route, but generally the sojourn is quiet.

A line-up of BLM recreation sites, open to camping and picnicking, extend riverside relaxation. A tributary waterfall and fishing platform enhance Alder Glen. Beyond Dovre, the road climbs out of the Nestucca River Canyon, so the drive backtracks to U.S. 101 to complete the return north to Tillamook. En route, 319-foot Munson Creek Falls, the tallest waterfall in the Coast Range, may beckon visitors aside; springtime offers the best viewing of these falls. Much of the time, the falls spill in tinsel-like streams.

LAND OF FALLING WATERS
Silver Falls Tour Route

Despite the urban pressures that accompany holding two-thirds of the state's population, the Willamette Valley still has the signature agricultural bounty that led the Oregon Trail pioneers to cross a continent. Fields of grass, whiffs of onion, plots of peppermint, rows of corn, waves of wheat, orderly orchards of fruit and nuts, berry patches, and slopes of wine grapes testify to the fulfillment of the promise. Red-tailed hawks soar through the skies, and in spring and fall, skeins of geese pass between feeding and roosting sites. At harvest time, stacked flats and crates edge the fields as farm workers bend over their tasks. Farm trucks brimming with produce share the road.

This drive through the valley cornucopia offers a bit of everything—Norman Rockwell towns, Bavarian oompah bands, a superb waterfall park, spiritual retreats, and a touchstone to yesteryear. Festivals celebrate everything from Bach to tulips, from bratwurst to tostadas. At the Aumsville Corn Festival, a fistful of napkins combats buttery fingers.

Woodburn kicks off the drive, sending travelers down its tree-shaded streets to the Jesse Settlemier House, the town founder's fourteen-room mansion, which is an interesting mix of Queen Anne, Craftsman, and Victorian architectural styles. A host of blooms, a rare American chestnut, and other stately trees complement this grand dame. A stroll through the graceful park-like grounds or a house tour will start off your road trip with yesteryear charm. The town's small museums or its Tulip Festival

ROUTE 3

This 55-mile signed route off Interstate 5 travels between exits 271 at Woodburn and 248 near Turner, passing through Mount Angel, Silverton, Sublimity, and Aumsville, staying mainly on Oregon Highway 214.

The fertile Willamette Valley attracted the Oregon pioneer west and its cornucopia is richly varied, including everything from pumpkins to peppermint, hazelnuts to hops, and strawberries to string beans. Produce stands and U-pick sites attract many backroads travelers.

Farmers in the Willamette Valley take to the fields early.

Oregon's oldest covered bridge, the Gallon House Bridge, spans Abiqua Creek in the Willamette Valley. The 1917-built bridge takes its name from a nearby house where bootleg whiskey was sold by the gallon during Prohibition.

FACING PAGE:
Silver Falls State Park is Oregon's largest state park and home to ten major waterfalls, including South Falls, the park's signature waterfall. South Falls plummets 177 feet and a trail takes hikers beneath the falls, offering a lookout through the droplet veil.

Willamette Valley U-pick/we-pick farms and produce-stands allow firsthand sampling of the harvest. They also can introduce visitors to scrumptious little-known fruit and vegetable varieties that never reach the market because they are too plump and juicy for shipping.

Ice-cream makers and jam and jelly companies will attest Oregon is the place for succulent berries of all kinds—strawberries, raspberries, blueberries, boysenberries, Marionberries, the works. Valley peaches burst with syrup and flavor, and the number of apple varieties will astound visitors. Cherries, pears, plums, apricots, and nectarines fill out a fruit salad. "U-pickers" can also snap peas, pick a pepper, or pluck an eggplant. Cucumbers, beans, tomatoes, corn, pumpkins, Oregon's famous hazelnuts, and walnuts swell the bounty. Produce-stands add fresh-pressed ciders, local jams, and honey. Diners feature fresh fruit pies and berry shortcakes.

Although the selected valley routes string past some of these sites, side roads hold new discoveries and are typically quieter than the main roads. Hazelgreen and Silverton Roads offer opportunities away from Oregon Highway 214. Hand-lettered signs for U-pick farms can cue a detour. Travelers can also uncover locations through area newspapers—in the regularly printed produce calendars or in the classified ads for "farm and garden" or "food and produce."

(mid March to mid April) can stretch out your acquaintance with Woodburn.

Once Oregon Highway 214 takes over as guide, your five senses will all say country. This drive shows-off a good many of the 161 crops grown in the valley. Conifer rows partition the valley plat of grasses, orchards, cane berries, nuts, and hops (those peculiar vines climbing between what seem to be planted rows of telephone posts). Valley oaks add a lovely complement, and fruit stands abound.

The Bavarian roots of Mount Angel are unmistakable, from the Bavarian-style business shields to the bratwurst, sauerkraut, and taps of beer. Murals and art capture the lighthearted aspect of the community. Festivities peak with Oktoberfest (beginning the second Thursday after Labor Day). Founded by Benedictine monks, Mount Angel also has a spiritual side, with Mount Angel Abbey, which sits atop a hill in town, and the more centrally located Queen of Angels Monastery, the historic campus of the Benedictine Sisters who later followed the monks here.

Silverton, gateway to Silver Falls State Park and home of the Oregon Garden, has an easy charm of bygone days. Setting the town's mood are its tree-lined streets, vintage homes, family parks, murals depicting the town's history, and babbling creek through town. At Silverton Reservoir, grandfathers and grandsons still talk as they row and cast.

The Oregon Garden extends a peaceful backdrop for a casual stroll. Opened in 2001, it is a growing attraction; its 70 cultivated acres will one day quadruple. The garden includes a remarkable 400-year-old valley oak.

Charming floral and shrub displays, fountains, sculptures, ponds, wetlands, and woods shape the retreat. Interlocking paths, a tram, and frequent benches allow visitors to set their own pace.

Birds and butterflies also enjoy the Oregon Garden, including an undaunted swallow attracted to the giant dragonfly sculpture in the Children's Garden. While the playfulness of the Children's Garden appeals to all ages, the Gordon House, a separate attraction, is best for adults. Oregon's only Frank Lloyd Wright–designed house, it barely escaped demolition—what the Wright Conservancy called its closest call. Saving the home required relocating it to its present site. Although a modest structure, the architectural line and the uses of light and form speak to Wright's vision. The home's uncanny fit into its new setting remains true to a Wright design.

Silver Falls is the largest of Oregon's state parks and, many would argue, its finest; it was once considered for national park status. In the park's Silver Creek Canyon sits a gallery of ten major waterfalls, ranging from 27 to 178 feet high, with half exceeding 100 feet high. Erosion by Silver Creek carved out the cliffs, caverns, and amphitheater bowls that display the waterfalls. South Falls is the most frequently photographed, but each waterfall is splendid in its canyon and forest backdrop. The park's historic lodge, picnic areas, campground, and big trees amplify its welcome.

From the rich shade of the park, the route twists south and down into the valley, with its bright light, century-old farms, and small agricultural communities. More of the same greets travelers once across Highway 22, which joins Interstate 5 at Salem, offering an opportunity to shorten the tour. Hand-lettered signs for brown eggs, Polled Herefords, and free kittens may dot the final distance. At Turner, the 1891 king-size Memorial Tabernacle, on the National Register of Historic Places, causes heads to turn. Then, it's back to Interstate 5 and the real world.

ALL THINGS COASTAL
Pacific Coast Scenic Byway, Central Section

ROUTE 4

This route is a 106-mile sample of the Pacific Coast Scenic Byway, which follows U.S. Highway 101 from the Columbia River to the California border; this snapshot runs between Lincoln City and Reedsport.

Oregon's coast is legendary, with its sandy strands, rocky headlands, rumpled dunes, tide pools, and an always mesmerizing surf. Nesting seabirds, bald eagles, sea lions, spouting gray whales, and even the occasional orca endorse the stage. But the coast's invitation extends beyond its natural offerings, with a rich maritime lore, fun-in-the-sun coastal shops, salty bay fronts, chainsaw art, battling kites, and castles in the sand.

In 1913, Oregon Governor Oswald West declared the coastal beaches to be highways—an action that kept the sandy strands public and undeveloped. Historically, the beaches were the lone transportation links between isolated coastal communities, and they were used by both Native

At Silver Falls State Park, the 7.5-mile Trail of Ten Falls, sometimes referred to as the Silver Creek Canyon Trail, takes hikers past a stunning gallery of waterfalls. The 106-foot Middle North Falls is among the most lovely.

TOP:

In time for Easter, the Wooden Shoe Bulb Company near Woodburn bursts out with daffodil and tulip blooms. Visitors are welcome to stroll the display garden and field paths.

BOTTOM:

In Woodburn, the stately Jesse Settlemier House, home of the town founder, invites visitors to tour its rooms or stroll the attractive park-like grounds. Several of the small towns on the Silver Falls Tour Route boast picturesque old homes.

Americans and pioneers. Beachgoers today reap the benefits of West's action—363 miles of unprecedented access to natural shores. Some beaches have shell fossils (Moolack Beach), some have agates (Lost Creek), and some are untrammeled canvases.

Lincoln City launches this trip. This linear town incorporates five former beach communities. It is known for its spring and fall kite festivals and for its winter treasure hunts for blown-glass floats hidden on the beaches. By contrast, its little sister to the south, Depoe Bay, is a compact seafront village, where fishing and whale-watching charters enjoy a quick hop to the open ocean through the world's smallest port.

State parks, beaches, and waysides pepper the length of the coast, allowing frequent stops and tastes of the sea breeze. The ocean mirrors the weather; it can be as striking blue as the sky, or as moody and mysterious as the fog. Wind is common at any time; the best weather comes in fall.

Newport's waterfront smacks of the sea, with circling gulls, barking sea lions, stacked crab rings, and old warehouses. A series of marine-inspired murals and an inviting seawalk further put visitors in a nautical mood. The historic fishing village remains home to one of Oregon's largest commercial fishing fleets, and tuna still can be bought fresh off the boat. For alternative windows to the sea, visitors may look to the Oregon Coast Aquarium and Mark O. Hatfield Marine Science Center.

Named after the Indian tribe, the small town of Yaquina in Lincoln County rests along Yaquina Bay; this is how the town looked while under construction in 1891. In the late 1800s, stage passengers traveled from the Willamette Valley to a point near here and then completed the journey to the coast via the river bay. (Courtesy of Salem Public Library)

What would a visit to the coast be without foghorns and lighthouses? Newport boasts a pair of lighthouses. The Yaquina Bay Light, on the harbor in town, was used only three years but comes complete with ghost story. Its replacement, the 1873 Yaquina Head Light (at the north end of town), shines over Yaquina Head Outstanding Natural Area; it is the tallest of Oregon's nine remaining lighthouses, standing 93 feet tall.

Off Yaquina Head sits Colony Rock, a nesting site for thousands of common murres, Brandt's and pelagic cormorants, and pigeon guillemots. April through July, it's standing room only for the colony; nesting gulls prefer the headland cliff. The headland also serves leviathan seekers. Some twenty-six species of whale have been spied offshore, but gray whales account for 95 percent of sightings.

Tiny Yachats boasts one of Oregon's more spectacular rock-and-sea clashes. At Smelt Sands State Recreation Site, fingers of jet-black basalt confront the white fury of the sea in high-spraying spectacle. Winter storms feed the fury, and thunder rumbles in the chests of onlookers.

To the south looms Cape Perpetua, named by Captain James Cook in 1778. Cape Perpetua Scenic Area encompasses this rugged headland, wild coast, forest, and 22 miles of hiking trails. Adjoining Cummins Creek Wilderness to the south, the scenic area shapes a large open space for wildlife. The summit's Whispering Spruce Trail links two stonework vantages built by the Civilian Conservation Corps. Shoreline attractions Devils Churn, Cooks Chasm, and Spouting Horn live up to their provocative names.

The signature flashes of Heceta Head Lighthouse call travelers south. Its stunning coastal perch makes this the state's most photographed lighthouse. Two-hundred-foot cliffs, the rocky cove of Devils Elbow, and the sea-battered Conical and Parrot Rocks shape the light's dominion. The associated lightkeeper's house doubles as a visitor center and a bed and breakfast.

Raucous barks announce the nearness of the Steller sea lion rookery at privately held Sea Lion Caves. According to the owners, this gaping 12-story-high cavern spans the length of a football field—plenty of room for beasts that can weigh 1 ton each. An elevator sinks 208 feet to the cave floor for viewing this wildlife spectacle. Elsewhere along the coast, smaller, more common California sea lions frequent docks and waterfronts, and harbor seals sun themselves on isolated rocks.

Wrapping up the journey, the cities of Florence and Reedsport shape the northern gateway to Oregon Dunes National Recreation Area, which stretches nearly 50 miles between Florence and Coos Bay. The origin of the dunes traces back 7,000 years. Over time, sand slowly eroded from the interior mountains and rode the rivers to the sea, where currents distributed the deposits along the shoreline. At the end of the last ice age, a bulldozing wave action pushed the sand to shore. Centuries of wind then finessed the shifting landscape. The resulting curvaceous dunes can reach heights of 400 feet. Cedar trail-posts guide hikers across the loose sand to the beach. Besides its well-publicized

Fishing was a primary industry for coastal settlers, but before them, the native peoples relied on the bounty of the sea. At Newport, in 1900, the Rock Oyster Queen carried on the tradition of her people. (Courtesy of Salem Public Library)

BRIDGES

Architecturally, Oregon's coastal bridges are among the nation's finest, and eligible for the National Register of Historic Places. Many spans on the Pacific Coast Scenic Byway were built in the 1920s and 1930s, the vision of Conde B. McCullough, master bridge builder. His concept of bridge design combined aesthetics with function. Hallmarks of a McCullough bridge include soaring arches, dignified gateway spires, architectural railings, Art Deco pylons, and gothic columns. The results are civil-engineering landmarks.

Historic McCullough bridges in Astoria are the Old Youngs Bay Bridge and the Lewis and Clark River Bridge; Tillamook's representative is the Wilson River Bridge. A lineup of these photogenic concrete bridges begins at Depoe Bay and continues south along U.S. 101. Alsea Bay Bridge, the only McCullough bridge to have been replaced (in 1991), uses architectural pieces of the original in its new design.

ABOVE:

The view north from Roads End State Park in Lincoln City includes this popular walking beach, where beachcombers can find agates and sometimes a handsome blown-glass float.

RIGHT:

In Yaquina Head Outstanding Natural Area at the northern outskirts of Newport, Yaquina Head Lighthouse stands 93 feet tall. This popular attraction draws photographers, tourists, and wildlife enthusiasts. Offshore, Colony Rock offers the closest mainland viewing of nesting seabirds; whale watchers can spy the spouts of gray whales.

Along the old-time waterfront of Newport, nautical-themed murals adorn the warehouses and shops. Commercial fishing boats and fish markets are interspersed among the galleries, eateries, and shops.

BELOW:

A series of scenic bridges built in the 1930s dot the Pacific Coast Highway, and Cape Creek Bridge above Devils Elbow beach is one of them. The rolling arches are reminiscent of the Roman aqueducts.

vehicle areas, the recreation area encompasses natural beaches and dunes, teeming estuaries, and coastal lakes. These habitats support animals such as hummingbirds, deer, frogs, raccoons, and nesting plovers.

Reedsport doubles as the jump-off for Dean Creek Elk Viewing Area. A 3.5-mile detour east on Oregon Highway 38 finds the meadow frequented by eighty to one hundred Roosevelt elk, just one more jewel in the bottomless trove of the Oregon coast.

HEART OF THE VALLEY
Benton County Scenic Loop

ROUTE 5

From Benton County Courthouse in Corvallis, this 76-mile loop travels southward on Oregon Highway 99 West, turns west on Alpine Road, and adds a 10-mile spur to Alsea Falls, before heading north via Bellfountain Road, U.S. Highway 20/Oregon Highway 34, and Kings Valley Highway. Maxfield Creek Road and Airlie Road in neighboring Polk County take drivers back east to Highway 99 West.

In the shadow of Marys Peak (elevation 4,097 feet), the tallest peak in the Coast Range, this country drive rolls across valley farmland and foothill forest. Fittingly, it begins in Corvallis, which means "heart of the valley." Corvallis is a relaxed, friendly, rural college-town, with more than a dash of 1960s easy spirit and Oregon State University (OSU) beaver pride. College students make up nearly one-third of the town's population, contributing to its rural/progressive dynamic. Art galleries, theaters, a weekly farmers market (May through October), and a host of fine parks and bicycle paths speak of the town's values. The lovely 1888 Italianate courthouse—the oldest in Oregon still used as such—is an emblem for the drive.

South of Corvallis, Oregon 99 West enters the valley flatland of evergreen hedgerows, open fields, blueberry bushes, and wheeled irrigation lines. The tour passes the Georgian-style Willamette Grange (1923), before reaching the turnoff to 5,300-acre William L. Finley National Wildlife Refuge. Winter through spring, visitors can find Canada geese in the thousands darkening the sky; usually, a bald eagle is the culprit behind the sky show. Mostly, though, the geese feed and rest.

Oak-clad hills, open fields, ash lowlands, wetlands, and dense shrubs shape wildlife habitats. The refuge documents 212 bird species, plus mammals such as deer, otters, and beavers. The refuge also holds a remnant of the vanishing valley prairie. A gravel driving-route, hiking trails, the historic Fiechter farmhouse and barn, and boardwalks contribute to the story of the refuge. Later in the drive, Bruce and Finley roads, off Bellfountain Road, offer backdoor entrances to the refuge.

At the intersection of Alpine and Bellfountain roads, near rustic Alpine Market, travelers turn west, going to Alsea Falls Recreation Site via Alpine Road and the South Fork Alsea River National Back Country Byway. This part of the route transitions from valley farmland to tree farm to timberland. At Alsea Falls Recreation Site, visitors can picnic and camp beneath the 400-year-old trees along the South Fork Alsea River. A river falls, Alsea Falls arrives in a fanfare of cascades; Green Peak Falls, a tributary falls reached via foot trail, has a width rivaling its 50-foot height.

The loop resumes on Bellfountain Road, traversing valley foothills mottled by oaks and Christmas tree farms. Pastures of sheep, cows, horses, and llamas lend a pastoral element. This road is part of the historic Applegate Trail, a southern branch of the Oregon Trail that passed into northern California and up through southern Oregon. Bellfountain Park, off Dawson Road, is perfect for a big picnic lunch; here resides the nation's longest picnic table (85 feet), consisting of a single plank cut from a 422-year-old Douglas fir.

At Philomath, the route zigzags to follow U.S. 20/Oregon Highway 34 west. *Philomath* is Greek for "love of learning." The town of Philomath traces its beginning to a United Methodist institution of higher learning that served the entire Northwest from this spot in the mid 1800s. Benton County Historical Museum occupies what was the old college. Exhibits introduce tribal, settler, and timber history. The timber legacy is visible as traffic rushes travelers west to the quieter Kings Valley Highway and the next leg of the journey.

A quick turnoff at the start of the Kings Valley Highway leads a couple of miles to Harris Covered Bridge on the Tumtum River. A parking area precedes the bridge and is marked by a 500-year-old tree stump.

Back on the highway, the route wiggles north between rounded hills of lichen-dressed oaks and Douglas firs, coming to the marked turnoff to Fort Hoskins Historic Park. The park is the site of an early day fort on the Luckiamute River. Built in 1856, the fort had a dual purpose: guarding a key passage through the Coast Range and protecting the Siletz Indians on the newly formed Coast Reservation. Because the fort's usefulness waned during the Civil War, it was abandoned in 1865. Today, a flag flaps over the one-time parade ground and an interpretive trail rings the historic site, describing the fort, its function, and its place in military and Native American history.

On Maxfield Creek and Airlie roads, research forests and wineries are possible stops. Airlie serves up valley settings, adding distant views of Mount Jefferson and Three Sisters. A wild turkey just might cross the road. Highway 99 West then offers a fast return south to Corvallis. Marked turns for the E. E. Wilson Wildlife Area, Jackson-Frazier Wetlands, and Oregon State University's Peavy Arboretum and McDonald State Forest (living laboratories for research and education) offer a last chance for nature walks before returning to town.

WINERIES

Favored with ideal volcanic soils, a mild climate, and perfect elevation, Oregon's pinot noir and chardonnay grapes and wines have gained national and international recognition. Hillside, valley, and coastal locations showcase the lovingly tended vine-laced rows.

Although most of Oregon's wineries are small, family-run enterprises, the public is generally welcome. Vineyard paths, winery tours, and tasting rooms head up activities. Many vineyards host festivals, including some that couple jazz, bluegrass, or Highland pipes with the grape. Some provide attractive picnic areas, and most have nonalcoholic drinks for designated drivers.

The Oregon Tourism Commission puts out a detailed annual guide to Oregon's wineries. Brochures can be picked up at visitor centers, wineries, or other travel outlets, or they can be requested from the commission.

LEFT:
Country markets, such the Alpine Market on Benton County Scenic Loop, are popular places to stop for cold pop or ice cream while traveling Oregon's backroads.

BELOW:
Cascading Alsea Falls is the centerpiece to Alsea Falls Recreation Site, located in a lush Coast Range temperate rainforest.

Several covered bridges still span Crabtree and Thomas creeks in Linn County. The 103-foot-long Larwood Covered Bridge is the main attraction at a small picnic area on Crabtree Creek.

LEFT:
Linn County is largely rural, and picturesque farms and pastures are part of the scenery on the Covered Bridge Country Tour.

ABOVE:
The rich, thick grasses of Linn County make it ideal sheep country. The town of Scio hosts festivals that celebrate the sheep-rearing tradition.

Spans across Time
Covered Bridge Country Tour

East of Albany, this signed 43-mile Linn County tour loosely follows Oregon Highway 226 between Crabtree (2.75 miles east of the junction of Highway 226 and U.S. Highway 20) and Jordan (south of Lyons). Side roads lead to five bridges.

This trip writes the prescription to heal the harried. It exudes quiet country charm, with relaxed travel, pastoral scenes, babbling waters, and picturesque bridges. This is a drive for rolled-down windows and elbows in the breeze. Hay-fever sufferers should stick with the air conditioner, however—Linn County bills itself "the Grass Seed Capital of the World." Bird songs, wind rustling through the alders, the bellow of cattle, the bleat of sheep, and the cock-a-doodle-doo of roosters enliven the journey.

Arriving in Crabtree via U.S. 20, travelers should follow signs pointing north on Hungry Hill Road, the official starting point of the tour. The drive immediately enters the country spell: flowing fields, rustic barns, orchards and berry patches, and aisles of oak, alder, and cottonwood. Hand-lettered signs herald the sale of brown eggs, while cats stalk mice in the fields.

Before long, the drive reaches its first bridge, Hoffman Covered Bridge, circa 1936, spanning Crabtree Creek. Sporting a crisp white coat of paint and framed by Douglas fir and alder, the bridge is ready for a photograph. All five covered bridges on the route have nearby parking; just watch out for passing vehicles. Each bridge interior reveals a wooden Howe-truss construction, characterized by a series of half-A support timbers. Adze markings on this bridge's upper timbers indicate a hand-hewn construction. Bridge covers protect the trusses from rainy Oregon winters.

After a spell on Highway 226, Gilkey Road leads to the next classic white span, Gilkey Covered Bridge, which underwent reconditioning in 1998. Its mostly open sides look out on Thomas Creek. This covered bridge sits side-by-side with a railroad trestle bridge. Rail was the life artery to rural America in the late 1800s and early 1900s. Besides carrying products to market, railroads brought supplies and contact with the cities and nation beyond the farm. Robinson Drive returns travelers east to Highway 226.

Scio, home of the Scio Lamb and Wool Festival and sheep dog trials, is the biggest town on the tour, population 650. From its beginning as a flour mill, this quaint agricultural town has grown to include churches, a couple of diners, a market, and gas pumps. On the north bank of Thomas Creek, Chapin Park holds the Depot Museum (open weekends May through October, but the grounds can be explored anytime). Shade trees and picnic tables invite visitors to linger.

East of Scio, a crescent spur shaped by Richardson Gap Road and Shimanek Bridge Drive leads to Shimanek Covered Bridge. This newcomer, built in 1966, breaks the white color scheme with its red paint and white trim. It spans Thomas Creek and can be admired via gateway and side-angle views. Hannah Covered Bridge, off Highway 226 at Camp Morrison

Road, marks the turnaround site for the tour. It, too, spans Thomas Creek, which engages visitors' attention with treed banks and cobble bars. In spring, kayakers sometimes take out at the bridge. Swimmers likewise make use of the spot.

Larwood Park, southeast off Highway 226 via Richardson Gap Road and Larwood Drive, holds the fifth bridge. Quiet, cool, and attractive, this little park on Crabtree Creek makes an ideal spot for picnicking, viewing Larwood Covered Bridge, or splashing about in the creek. Roaring River swells Crabtree Creek at the park.

Passage through Larwood Covered Bridge leads back to Highway 226 via Fish Hatchery Drive. However, travelers may delay their return, following signs to either Roaring River Fish Hatchery or a U-pick/we-pick blueberry patch. Roaring River Fish Hatchery (1.2 miles off the tour) is open from 7:30 A.M. to 7:00 P.M. Interpretive signs and a kiosk introduce the facility, which rears 250,000 each of rainbow trout and steelhead and which has a display pond of sturgeon. The blueberry field sits 2 miles off the tour route. Berry-stained fingers are just the thing to top a day in the country.

Today, Hannah Covered Bridge stands alone, but in 1960, a general store was near the bridge, making the area a center of activity. (Courtesy of Salem Public Library)

PART II

THE NORTHERN CASCADES: VOLCANOES, FORESTS, AND WILD AND SCENIC WATERS

FACING PAGE:

Multnomah Falls is the showpiece of the Columbia River Gorge. Always in the top three of Oregon tourist attractions, the falls can be viewed from observation deck and trail. Benson Bridge crosses Multnomah Creek between Upper and Lower Multnomah Falls.

ABOVE:

Office Covered Bridge in Westfir was constructed to carry logging trucks across the North Fork of the Middle Fork Willamette River to a mill. At 180 feet in length, it is Oregon's longest covered bridge.

The Cascade Mountain Range—the primary divide in Oregon—is part of a string of sleeping volcanoes that stretch south from Mount Garibaldi in British Columbia to Mount Lassen in northern California. Volcanic activity shaped these mountains. Millions of years ago, the first eruptive sequence created the older western volcanoes. The more recent sequence (several thousand years ago) formed the younger eastern volcanoes. Mount Hood, Oregon's tallest peak, shoots 11,235 feet skyward, but the most amazing feature about the Cascade volcanoes is their vertical relief. They have pop-up-book surprise.

It was renowned botanist David Douglas, among the first to inventory the range's plants and animals, who dubbed these mountains "the Cascades." The Oregon Cascades separate the verdant Willamette Valley from the Columbia Plateau and the eastern high deserts. Vegetation varies by latitude, elevation, and slope. The western slopes show a primary cover of Douglas fir and western hemlock; the eastern slopes typically wear ponderosa and lodgepole pine. Deer, elk, coyotes, raccoons, and other furry denizens inhabit the forests. Bird sightings can include the bald eagle, osprey, spotted owl, and Clark's nutcracker.

The mountains represent a four-season vacationland, which can fill a dance card with activities from mountain climbing to rafting to huckleberry picking. Downhill and Nordic skiing, snowshoeing, snowmobiling, and even sled-dog racing engage winter sports enthusiasts. If it takes place outdoors and is fun, the Cascades have it. High lakes, meadows, sterling rivers, waterfalls, and rock outcroppings punctuate the offering. The incredible beauty is available to windshield viewer and hiker alike.

Small towns with timber and recreational underpinnings dot the mountain routes. Nearly all have a service aspect, as the towns reinvent themselves with the uncertainty of logging. Forest management plays a strong role in several communities; nearly everyone has an opinion on it. By pulling up a chair at a diner or sharing the time of day at a general store, travelers learn a bit about the people. Billboards and posters hint at their humor.

HAIL COLUMBIA!
Historic Columbia River Highway

ROUTE 7

West-to-east travel on the Historic Columbia River Highway (U.S. Highway 30) begins at exit 18 off Interstate 84. The second leg of the route starts at the interstate's exit 69 at Mosier. The total trip, ending in The Dalles, measures 71 miles. It is not recommended for trailers or large RVs.

One of the prettiest drives in the country, this historic highway pursues the Columbia River, twisting along the towering basalt cliffs of the Oregon shore. An ancient, roiling Columbia River carved out this impressive chasm between Oregon and Washington. The nearly perpendicular cliffs stretch 3,000 feet skyward. Streaking the walls are more than a dozen major waterfalls and a springtime complement of unnamed falls. The western part of the Columbia River Gorge National Scenic Area presents a sylvan setting of Douglas fir and bigleaf maple; the eastern gorge consists of arid grassy steppes.

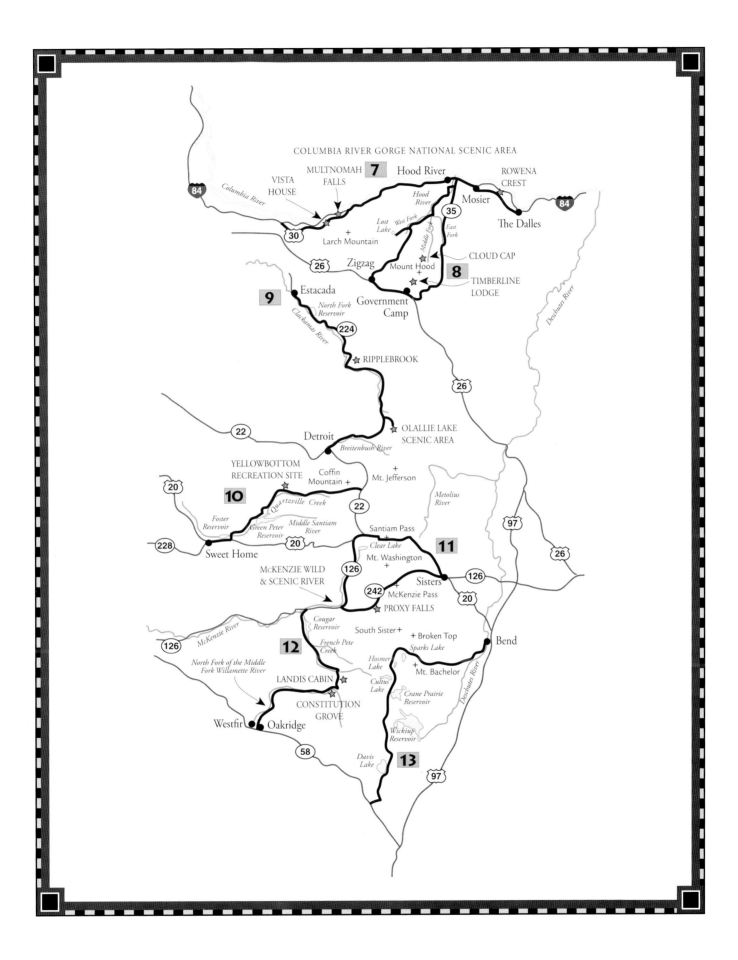

COLUMBIA RIVER GORGE NATIONAL SCENIC AREA

MULTNOMAH FALLS **7** Hood River

ROWENA CREST

VISTA HOUSE

84

Columbia River

Hood River

Mosier

The Dalles

84

West Fork

Lost Lake

35

East Fork

Middle Fork

30

+ Larch Mountain

CLOUD CAP

26

Zigzag

Mount Hood **8**

+

TIMBERLINE LODGE

Deschutes River

9 Estacada

North Fork Reservoir

Government Camp

Clackamas River

224

26

RIPPLEBROOK

22

Detroit

OLALLIE LAKE SCENIC AREA

Breitenbush River

YELLOWBOTTOM RECREATION SITE

Coffin Mountain +

+ Mt. Jefferson

Metolius River

20

10

Quartzville Creek

97

Foster Reservoir

Green Peter Reservoir

Middle Santiam River

Santiam Pass

228

22

Clear Lake

11

Sweet Home

20

126

Mt. Washington +

26

McKENZIE WILD & SCENIC RIVER

126

242

Sisters

126

McKenzie Pass

20

126

McKenzie River

PROXY FALLS

Cougar Reservoir

South Sister +

+ Broken Top

Bend

12

French Pete Creek

Sparks Lake

North Fork of the Middle Fork Willamette River

Hosmer Lake

+ Mt. Bachelor

Deschutes River

LANDIS CABIN

Cultus Lake

Crane Prairie Reservoir

CONSTITUTION GROVE

Westfir Oakridge

58

Wickiup Reservoir

Davis Lake

13

97

FACING PAGE:

The Oregon white oak grassland blankets the flat terraces of the Columbia River Gorge, adding to scenery along the route. In the Columbia River Gorge National Scenic Area, private lands intersperse public lands.

ABOVE:

The picturesque Historic Columbia River Highway is complemented by Italianate stonework side railings, built by the Civilian Conservation Corps. The characteristic vertical basalt cliffs of the Gorge are breathtaking.

LEFT:

Bridal Veil Creek races in cascades to join the Columbia River. Bigleaf maples lean over the water, showering the creek with leaves in autumn.

The route pairs with the Sandy River and rolling rural countryside before entering the gorge. Fishing and smelt dipping (when runs are good) are popular Sandy River pursuits. True to the "backroads" idea, the historic highway necessitates slow travel and has ample viewpoints and trailheads for stepping into nature.

Portland Women's Forum State Park and, to its east, Vista House, shape the gateway to the gorge. The park's vantage serves up the icon image: an upstream view of the gorge with Vista House prominent atop Crown Point. The point is a National Natural Landmark, elevation 733 feet. Vista House, a round, two-story stone pavilion, recalling Thor's Crown from mythology, seems almost intended by nature. Visitor exhibits, a gift shop, and balcony viewing of a 30-mile gorge expanse further recommend a stop. Between the park and Vista House, drivers can take the 17.5-mile side road up Larch Mountain, which offers a top-of-the-gorge, three-volcano view.

Waterfalls and their companion trails appear one after another, starting with 249-foot Latourel Falls. Multnomah Falls, the nation's fourth tallest at 620 feet, remains the most popular. Legend has it that the spray cradles the face of an Indian maiden who plunged to her death. At the base sits the attractive 1925 stone wayside, Multnomah Lodge, with its visitor center, gift shop, restaurant, and concessions. In autumn, fingers point to the swishing red bodies of spawning salmon in Multnomah Creek.

Wahkeena Falls is perhaps the most graceful of the roadside waterfalls. It originates from an uphill spring and spills as a billowing horsetail plume. Tucked in a mossy crease, serene Shepperds Dell Falls served its original owners as a chapel, while the mossy slot of Oneonta Gorge enfolds a unique botanical area.

Past Ainsworth State Park, drivers have the option of returning directly to Interstate 84 or following the frontage road 2 miles to Interstate 84, adding a visit to John B. Yeon State Park. The park trail leads to a pair of waterfalls: Elowah and Upper McCord. Elowah is a study in elegance. The Upper McCord Falls viewpoint salutes the area's imposing cliffs as much as the beautiful waterfall.

On Interstate 84, marked turnoffs to Bonneville Dam, Eagle Creek Recreation Area, and Cascade Locks can call travelers aside. At each stop, the story of salmon unfolds. Historically, the abundance of salmon brought Native American tribes from across the region to fish and trade, making the gorge an important cultural center. Attractions at the dam are salmon-viewing windows and a counting station. Salmon still spawn in Eagle Creek, and during salmon runs, fishing poles stand at attention along Cascade

HISTORIC COLUMBIA RIVER HIGHWAY

The Historic Columbia River Highway represents the vision of Samuel C. Hill and the engineering of Samuel C. Lancaster. The route is a masterpiece of both nature and construction, and the elements seamlessly blend and complement each other at every corner. The historic highway's mossy, Italianate stonework bridges and railings, graceful hairpin turns, and framed views represent art as well as engineering. When the route opened in 1916, Model-T Fords were the car of the time, and the skinny curvaceous road served up grand views and high adventure. Theodore Roosevelt proclaimed the road the greatest piece of engineering in its day; the *Illustrated London News* dubbed it "the king of roads." It was the first scenic highway in America, and is now a landmark on the National Register of Historic Places.

Locks. Farther east, the Hood River entices with its fruit orchards and windsurfing.

On the historic highway's eastern segment, travelers enter another realm, one often dressed in golden hues. Oregon white oaks, and occasionally poison oak, interrupt the grassy terraces. Near the start of the highway, signs point the way to an additional segment of the old highway now open as a hiking and bicycling trail. It leads to Mosier Twin Tunnels, which frame attractive gorge views and hold a 1921 inscription stone left by snowbound travelers stranded here for nine days.

The premier overlook on the eastern drive is Rowena Crest Viewpoint, which provides convenient access to Tom McCall Nature Conservancy Preserve. The snaking hairpin turns to and from the viewpoint are as much a wonder as the view itself. The trail to McCall Point provides an even loftier aspect. Spring is the preserve's peak season. Some 1,250 native plants are found in the gorge, so the showcase is first-rate. Balsamroot, Columbia desert parsley, chocolate lily, and larkspur contribute to the parade from March into June.

A few maples grow roadside as the route twists east and eventually emerges at The Dalles near the Columbia Gorge Discovery Center. The Dalles has a rich history. Until Barlow Road was constructed around Mount Hood, this town marked the end of the overland Oregon Trail. Because the earliest pioneers faced a treacherous raft ride on the Columbia River to reach the Willamette Valley, some pioneers ended their quest here.

Ezra Meeker traveled the Oregon Trail in his youth and retraced his steps as a man of maturing years. He is shown at the "End of the Oregon Trail" celebration in The Dalles in 1906. The Dalles once marked the end of the overland route of the Oregon Trail. From there, settlers took a harrowing ride on the Columbia River to reach the Willamette Valley. Construction of the Barlow Road eventually extended the overland route to Oregon City. (Courtesy of Crook County Historical Society)

ROUNDING WY'EAST
Mount Hood–Lost Lake Loop

Regal Mount Hood is this route's centerpiece. Orchards of apple, cherry, and pear trees; winter sports areas; timberline settings of rock and ice; and uncut forests and timber harvests shape the viewing aisles. Side trips lead to trailheads, mountain lakes, vistas, historic sites, huckleberry patches, and wilderness. The Oregon Trail circumvented the imposing mountain via the grueling Barlow Road. A lightly managed trail off Oregon Highway 35 at Barlow Pass puts modern feet on this historic route.

Scarcely into the trip, a 1.7-mile spur leads to Panorama Point. This observation site offers a bold look at Mount Hood looming above the orderly fruit-producing valley; it is especially appealing during the cherry-blossom or fruit season. Fruit-stands on Highway 35 parade the tastes of the harvest.

Hood River has long been famous for its fruit growing and wheat farming. The once-notorious wind has boosted the economy, attracting sailboarders and the businesses that serve them. Flowing through the valley is the town's namesake, which originates on Mount Hood. In spring,

ROUTE 8

From the town of Hood River, this 110-mile route follows Oregon Highway 35 south to U.S. Highway 26 West. At Zigzag, it continues north on East Lolo Pass Road (Forest Road 18) up and over the west side of Mount Hood, coming out at Lost Lake Road (Forest Road 13). Turning to the left adds the Lost Lake visit; to the right leads to Dee and to roads north to Hood River. East Lolo Pass Road is unsuitable for trailers and RVs; both it and Forest Road 13 close in winter.

LEFT:

Mount Hood watches over Lost Lake and its pictur-esque forested basin. The lake is a popular destination for picnicking and camping; a trail rings the lake.

ABOVE:

The Mount Hood Railroad tourist train carries guests through the orchard country and forest of the Hood River Valley, traveling between Hood River and Parkdale. Rivers and volcanoes make for lively scenery along the way.

MOUNT HOOD

To the tribes of the Northwest, Mount Hood was known as "Wy'East." The early peoples witnessed the mountain's fiery upheaval of rock and boulder, with the last eruptions occurring in the late 1700s. Mount Hood remains classified as a semi-active volcano. Sulphurous fumaroles in the Devils Kitchen Area, elevation 10,200 feet, remind people that Mount Hood has an eruptive potential, despite its current sleep.

The first recorded sighting of this Oregon landmark came in 1792, during the Vancouver Expedition. Lieutenant William E. Broughton sighted the conical peak above the Willamette River mouth and named it for Royal Navy Admiral Samuel Hood. In 1805, Lewis and Clark also noted the mountain.

Mount Hood is the highest peak in Oregon, and the fourth tallest volcano in the Cascades (Washington's Mount Rainier, at 14,411 feet, is the tallest). Mount Hood takes top honors as the most-climbed glaciated peak in the United States. Five ridges and nearly a dozen glaciers beckon climbers. Climbing routes branch off the Civilian Conserva-

tion Corps–built Timberline Trail, which encircles the mountain at the 6,000-foot elevation. The most popular south-side climbing route is Hogsback, followed by Mazama. The latter is named for the Mazamas, a Portland-based mountaineering group, whose history has been tied to Mount Hood since 1894.

The first full ascent was achieved in 1845. In 1867, the first women reached the summit, attired in skirts, no less.

Since then, hundreds of thousands of climbers have successfully conquered the summit, but the climb is not for amateurs. Training and a Mount Hood–experienced leader are recommended. All routes to the summit are technical climbs, requiring helmet, crampons, ice axe, shovel, climbing harness, and rope. Ascents begin at midnight and take place from May to mid July; the timing reduces the risks of avalanche and rockfall and ensures better footing. Besides the mountain's challenge, bitter cold, high winds, and changeable weather confront climbers.

Oregon waters have always attracted fishing enthusiasts. This pair is trying their luck on the Zigzag River in Mount Hood National Forest. (Courtesy of the United States Forest Service)

the churning, milky-gray waters betray their glacial origin. County and USFS campgrounds and trails provide closer looks at the river. But just as travelers settle into the quiet spell of the valley, Mount Hood jumps out with a "gotcha" kind of view.

At Parkdale Junction, a pair of small museums and Mount Hood Railroad bid visitors to take a 3-mile detour. Farther south, the Cloud Cap turnoff offers a chance for an up-close acquaintance with Mount Hood. This is one of the state's finest wilderness areas that can be reached by car. Parking lies 12.5 miles off Highway 35, ascending paved and gravel roads to the spectacular high-mountain setting. Mount Hood views, historic Cloud Cap Inn (no accommodations), and a timberline campground reward travelers. Timberline Trail encircles the mountain, revealing glacial till, ice, alpine meadow, and tortured tree-line vegetation.

Near the junction of Highway 35 and U.S. 26 sits the Pioneer Woman's Grave, discovered when the roads were built. Here, an unknown woman from the Oregon Trail was buried in the bed of a wagon; the hitch served as her grave marker. Modern tourists leave token stones, bundles of grass, and rustic crosses.

U.S. 26 is the hurried leg of the journey, owing to the year-round recreation opportunities along it and its easy proximity to Portland. Trillium Lake and Mirror Lake are popular with photographers. The blue platters toss back still-water reflections of Mount Hood and the bordering meadow and forest. Timberline Lodge (a 6-mile detour) offers Mount Hood accommodations. This lodge, built by the Civilian Conservation Corps, consists of natural building materials and showcases the fine masonry, woodwork, and carvings of master craftsmen. The lodge extends access to a winter and summer ski area and the 40-mile Timberline Trail. Springtime is delayed at 6,000 feet, with blooms arriving in late summer.

At the turn for East Lolo Pass Road, a 3-mile detour west on U.S. 26 leads to the Mount Hood Visitor Center, where travelers can inquire about the pass road and pick up travel materials. The well-used, winding, paved and gravel East Lolo Pass Road reveals the working mountain. Utility lines cross the mountain here, and various stages of logging make a patchwork of the slope. Through it all, Mount Hood remains an engaging host. Rhododendron, fireweed, and huckleberry decorate the clear-cut areas, and red-tailed hawks and flickers claim the sky. Where the road splits at the pass, Forest Road 18 bears right.

At Lost Lake Road (Forest Road 13), travelers head left to Lost Lake. Stories of this idyllic hidden lake had long been known, but it took an 1880 expedition of settlers from Hood River to discover its whereabouts. The triangular lake sits at the northern foot of Mount Hood and mirrors the peak's beauty. A campground, picnic area, and rustic resort, where cabins and rowboats can be rented, occupy the shoreline woods. Old-growth firs and cedars, rhododendrons, huckleberry bushes, and beargrass contribute to the postcard offering.

A trail, much of it boardwalk or otherwise handicap accessible, rings the lake. Another boardwalk explores the old-growth habitat. Above the lake, Lost Lake Butte rewards the ascent with a lofty aspect of Mount Hood, the Hood River Valley, and the surrounding forest.

The loop's return to Hood River follows Forest Road 13 east to the old timber mill community of Dee, reaching Dee Highway upon crossing the river. Signs point the way north to Hood River. An alternative route is to proceed to Parkdale and then on to Highway 35, taking it north.

ON THE WESTERN SLOPE
West Cascades Scenic Byway, Clackamas-Breitenbush Section

Part of the greater West Cascades Scenic Byway, this journey strings between Mount Hood National Forest and Willamette National Forest, following the Clackamas and Breitenbush rivers. A spur to 11,000-acre Olallie Lake Scenic Area completes this Cascades capsule. River segments reveal cliffs, canyons, big trees, rhododendrons, and deep pools. The scenic area's meadows and forests teem with clear mountain lakes. The combined trip was made for a fishing pole, picnic basket, and berry bucket. Although

The Portland-based Mazamas Mountain Club, shown here in 1963, is the leading authority on Mount Hood climbs. (Courtesy of the United States Forest Service)

ROUTE 9

This 70-mile route follows Oregon Highway 224 and Forest Road 46 between Estacada and Detroit. A departure from Forest Road 46, on paved and gravel Forest Roads 4690 and 4220 adds a 27-mile roundtrip to Olallie Lake Scenic Area. Forest Road 46 closes in winter.

RIGHT:

U.S. Forest Service campgrounds offer rustic overnight retreats along many of the backroads tours. Humbug Campground makes a great base from which to explore the West Cascades Scenic Byway.

ABOVE:

Pacific rhododendron, which blooms in late spring, is a common understory plant in the Mount Hood National Forest.

RIGHT:

Old-growth forest both houses and purifies the sparkling waters of Roaring Creek, which flows into the South Fork Breitenbush River. A national recreation trail parallels the river, crossing Roaring Creek.

Olallie Lake reflects Mount Jefferson in the morning calm. Olallie Lake Scenic Area is peppered with lakes, a mid-elevation Cascade Mountains forest, and cinder buttes.

campgrounds and trailheads are never far off, the only service communities are at the trip's ends: Estacada and Detroit.

Oregon is richly endowed with great rivers and the Clackamas is no exception. This bending beauty, which bears the name of a Chinookan tribe, includes fast riffles, deep pools, mossy boulders, gravel bars, and glassy stills. The river is noted for its fly-fishing, steelhead fishing, and spring kayaking. Near Estacada, a dam captures the Clackamas and forms North Fork Reservoir, where boating, camping, and lake recreation are available at utility-owned Promontory Park.

Oregon Highway 224 pairs with the river and provides access to ample turnouts, campgrounds, and picnic areas for safe river viewing and recreation. Maples, firs, mixed shrubs, blackberries, and wildflowers vary roadside views. Areas of old growth mottle the slopes, with lichen and stonecrop adorning the chunky cliffs of basalt. Side routes shoot off to lakes and trails.

Along the free-flowing river, three trails invite exploration: the 7.8-mile Clackamas River Trail, the 4.6-mile Riverside National Recreation Trail, and the 1-mile Alder Flat Trail, which ends at a roadless, wild stretch of the Clackamas River. About midway on the Clackamas River Trail, a spur briefly pursues Pup Creek upstream to a vista of Pup Creek Falls, a surprisingly long vertical drop that would be a major attraction in most states. The Riverside Trail pursues the Oak Grove Fork and main stem of the Clackamas River, passing among stunning big trees. On Alder Flat Trail, 250-year-old conifers brush the sky 150 feet above the trail; the alders are found riverside.

The Clackamas River Trail runs between Indian Henry and Fish Creek Campgrounds, while Rainbow and Riverside Campgrounds border either side of the Riverside Trail. Alder Flat Trail is just west of the old Ripplebrook Ranger Station.

Well-loved Olallie Lake Scenic Area (open mid June through September), at the base of Mount Jefferson, is a wilderness peppered with lakes. "Olallie" means berries; both huckleberry and blueberry bushes grow here. The scenic area further engages visitors' attentions with high-elevation meadows, mixed forests of true firs and lodgepole pines, a bumpy skyline of cinder buttes, and an intricate web of trails, including the Pacific Crest Trail. Along with Mount Jefferson, Olallie Butte stands watch over the lakes. Only pesky mosquitoes can dampen the offering.

Olallie and Monon lakes, the two biggest lakes in the area, occupy the heart of the scenic region. On Olallie Lake, a rustic resort rents cabins and rowboats. In 2001, lightning strikes sparked fires that swept parts of these lakeshores, but the bronzed, blackened, and silvered trees only add to the aura. New growth lends contrast.

Not be outdone, the area's many smaller lakes enchant visitors with blue waters, hidden locations, and solitude—at times, visitors can have a lake to themselves. Some lakes are popular for fishing; others for relaxing. Foot trails string the lakes together like blue beads.

The Breitenbush River later pairs with the byway, but is often hidden by steep vegetated banks. At times, the river channel is gorge-like. A few turnouts and campgrounds allow for viewing, but mostly, the forested travel aisle holds center stage. In June, rhododendron and a few dogwood blooms complement the mixed conifer-deciduous bower. Autumn sprinkles yellow and scarlet leaves at the feet of the evergreens.

South Breitenbush Gorge and its 2.5-mile national recreation trail suggest a side trip east off Forest Road 46 onto Forest Road 4685. The trail wanders among towering and wind-snapped old-growth trees as it pursues the South Fork Breitenbush River. Where a tight chasm (300 feet long, 10 feet wide, and 30 to 40 feet deep) contains the river, water gathers in a roiling fury. The unified image of white water and mossy cliffs is camera-worthy.

Closer to Detroit, the Breitenbush swells into the Breitenbush River Arm of Detroit Reservoir, and marinas come into view. Detroit Reservoir is one of the most popular motor-boating destinations in the state. The timber-tourist town of Detroit caps the journey.

IT ALL BEGINS AT HOME, SWEET HOME
Quartzville National Back Country Byway

ROUTE 10

This route travels through a historic mining district that yielded gold and silver from the late 1800s to about 1900, and then again during the Great Depression. Quartzville takes its name from the quartz formation at the mines, but time has erased all evidence of the town and the era. The one-time tent city with its few frame structures has returned to nature and sits on private land. Still, people smitten with "gold fever" can pan the gravels in a designated section of sparkling Quartzville Creek.

The canyon's riches today are its spectacular settings and scenic waters; the lower part of Quartzville Creek is a national wild and scenic river. Pockets of old-growth trees and outcrop cliffs send eyes soaring. Seasonally, Douglas iris, rhododendrons, and autumn foliage color the passageway. Ospreys, bald eagles, and Harlequin ducks may make appearances.

Situated along the old Santiam Wagon Road (part of the Oregon Trail), Sweet Home is a small, mural-decorated timber and agricultural town. The murals commemorate Native Americans, haying, and old-time logging. Weddell Covered Bridge in town can also delay visitors, as can an 8-mile detour north to McDowell Creek County Park, a place of falling waters, picnic grounds, and trails. County and BLM campgrounds and day-use areas offer spots to pause along the byway.

Heading up the tour are a pair of reservoirs: Foster and Green Peter. Foster Reservoir precedes the official BLM byway, while the emerald deep of Green Peter Reservoir stretches along the byway for 10 miles. Both impoundments appeal to boaters, anglers, and fun-in-the-sun seekers. Because summers can attract a lively reservoir crowd, seekers of nature's quiet typically prefer off-season travel.

This 50-mile route travels between U.S. Highway 20 (east of Sweet Home) and Oregon Highway 22 (east of Detroit). Starting from the junction of U.S. 20 and Oregon Highway 228 in Sweet Home, drivers head east on U.S. 20, turning north onto the marked byway in 5.7 miles. The route is not recommended for large RVs, and winter snow closes the higher reaches.

East of the Cascade Crest, ponderosa pines shape a primary climax forest. The mature trunk's golden-orange color wins the pine the nickname "yellow-belly;" other characteristics are the jigsaw-like bark and a vanilla or butterscotch scent. These pines reside along the Metolius Wild and Scenic River in Deschutes National Forest.

Autumn tints the vine maples and shrubs along the North Santiam River in Willamette National Forest.

Upper Proxy Falls and its companion, Lower Proxy Falls, each plummet 200 feet and are easily reached by a popular hike in the Three Sisters Wilderness. Lava flow and forest shape the falls environment.

Foster, a 3.5-mile-long blue oval, reflects the low hill above it. Green Peter captures the Middle Fork Santiam River and Quartzville Creek, with the Quartzville arm tucked in a stunning canyon confinement. Spring and summer steelhead migrate upstream, passing through ladders and elevators at dams. Fish viewing is possible on the South Santiam River below Foster Dam and at South Santiam Fish Hatchery. For many, though, Quartzville Creek is the true star. This enthralling, winding guide lures travelers upstream through its tight canyon and rock-and-tree settings to its headwaters. Across the pass, the drive switches character, revealing mountainsides of maturing and harvest forest.

Swift riffles, boulder cascades, and deep pools punctuate Quartzville Creek, but a steep bank usually denies easy access. Dogwood Recreation Site (day use) and Yellowbottom Recreation Site offer the main approaches. Douglas fir, cedar, hemlock, maple, dogwood, and alder frame the waterway and fashion a pleasing bower for the road. Bridges crisscross the creek. Upstream, the banks of the creek turn gorge-like, and the creek bed rests far below the road. In parts of the corridor, wildfires and floods have altered the forest tapestry.

As the route descends to Highway 22, it swings a broad arc around descriptively named Coffin Mountain. Mid-June showings of rhododendron, beargrass, and late-summer huckleberries (bigleaf, red, oval leaf, and Alaskan) soften the harshness of cut areas. Views stretch beyond the corridor to Coffin Mountain, Mount Jefferson, and Three Fingered Jack. Periodic signs point out turns to forest trails, including one up Coffin Mountain. This 1.5-mile trail climbs steeply to the box-like summit, its lookout, and a 360-degree view.

West on Highway 22 is Detroit; east is Sisters.

VOLCANO CENTRAL
McKenzie Pass–Santiam Pass Scenic Byway

ROUTE 11

From Sisters, this 82-mile circuit links Oregon Highway 242 (open July through October) with Oregon Highway 126 and U.S. Highway 20 (both open year-round). Off U.S. 20 is Forest Road 14, a must-see spur into the Metolius River Recreation Corridor.

The adjective for this drive is "spectacular." This central Cascades route showcases stunning volcanoes, two wilderness areas, wild and scenic rivers, some impressive waterfalls, and magnificent Clear Lake. The 75 square miles of lava flows, craters, and cinder cones speak to the area's fiery beginnings. Ponderosa pines, western larches, aspens, and old-growth Douglas firs vary the forest tapestry. The ample trailheads, viewpoints, and campgrounds allow visitors to step into the bounty.

At the junction of U.S. 20 and Oregon Highway 242, on the west side of Sisters, sits the East Portal information wayside—the chosen start. The route begins and ends at Sisters, a picturesque tourist and agricultural town with an 1880s western-frontier facade. There, shop windows display western sculpture and art, brightly colored quilts, handcrafted log furniture, and a bonanza of sundries. Sisters City Park offers creek-side picnicking and camping.

Llamas share the Three Sisters volcano backdrop as Highway 242 rolls south. The beginning of the route is straightforward, touring areas of ponderosa pine, gradually adding firs and twists with the climb. It then traces the crooked boundary between the Mount Washington and Three Sisters wilderness areas. At the close range afforded by the drive, the volcanic sisterly trio and the pointed helmet of Mount Washington rise up imposingly. In fall, the red and scarlet leaves of vine maples add touches of color to the sharp, hardened sea of the lava flow.

Dee Wright Observatory, Scott Lake, and Proxy Falls are the most popular stops on Highway 242, but any turnout or trail will satisfy with scenic beauty. The Pacific Crest Trail threads across the forbidding lava near Dee Wright Observatory. This round fortress built of lava seems to have risen from the flow. Its windows of odd shape and size pinpoint the volcanic landmarks. The locator compass on the open roof likewise identifies the neighborhood. In fall, crossbills may flock at the observatory, harvesting seeds from the conifers that surround the lava flow. A paved path travels atop the flow for a closer look at the 1,500-year-old lava. A few silvered snags and tortured trees rise among the appendages of melted rock.

At the base of Scott Mountain, shallow Scott Lake is a favorite for its Three Sisters reflections, quiet lake recreation, camping, and network of trails that top Scott Mountain and that visit several lakes. Proxy Falls Trail visits a pair of waterfalls showing nature's sleight-of-hand. In this ultimate bottomless-glass trick, a pair of 200-foot waterfalls plummets to dead-end pools that never overflow. (I could tell readers that the explanation rests with the porous lava, but I believe the illusion is more fun.)

Where the loop follows Highway 126, travelers enter the house of Clear Lake and the McKenzie Wild and Scenic River, and boy, what a house! Here, big Douglas firs and hemlocks shape a strong visual aisle. Clear Lake, created by a lava blockage and fed by Great Spring, is the dazzling, chilly (too cold for swimming) lake at the river's headwater. Remnants of the forest that drowned 3,000 years ago remain preserved 100 feet underwater. The water's remarkable clarity offers a window to this ancient forest. A picturesque forest-and-flow setting encompasses the lake. A trail around the lake shows off the place, its ospreys, and mergansers. A picnic area and rustic resort occupy the west shore. The resort serves up titan-size cinnamon rolls and also rents rowboats and cabins.

The acclaimed McKenzie River unfurls in spectacular dark pools, blue-ice cascades, bubbling eddies, and two major waterfalls: 63-foot Koosah

ABOVE:

Shallow Scott Lake serves up bold views of North and Middle Sisters, two of the Three Sisters. Tucked between the Mount Washington and Three Sisters Wilderness Areas, the lake offers picnicking and primitive camping and serves as a hub to wilderness trails.

RIGHT:

The quiet curvaceous route of Robert Aufderheide Memorial Drive sets a slow pace for admiring the rich bordering forest. This route parallels three waterways, the North Fork of the Middle Fork of the Willamette River, Roaring Creek, and the South Fork McKenzie River.

Landis Cabin recalls the early days of forest management, when rangers were stationed in the outback to address such concerns as trail management, fire fighting, and grazing.

The town of Sisters, known for its frontier atmosphere and charming shops and galleries, is also known for the llama ranches that sur-round it.

The great lightning fire of 2003—the B&B Complex Fire—consumed more than 90,000 acres in Deschutes and Willamette National Forests; evidence of the blaze lingers along U.S. Highway 20. Although the fire caused the evacuation of Camp Sherman, heroic efforts of firefighters spared both the town and the Metolius Wild and Scenic River corridor it borders. Normally, the blackened slopes fulfill nature's cycle to restore forest health. The extreme results here are the outcome of years of fire suppression. Fire is an agent to good forest health, scouring out debris, culling trees, killing insects and disease, opening seeds, and returning nutrients to the soil. Fire suppression allows the fuel base to get out of control, resulting in hot, fast, sweeping fires that are more destructive than beneficial.

(reached at Ice Cap Campground) and 100-foot Sahalie (0.2 mile to its north). Both falls can be reached by driving, but hikers and mountain bikers may prefer taking the McKenzie River National Recreation Trail, a 26-mile trail that pursues the river downstream from its origin to the community of McKenzie Bridge (a second byway portal). A favorite hiking loop travels the national recreation trail and the Falls Trail to encircle the waterfall duo, passing between the upper bridge and Carmen Reservoir. Numerous cascades add to the viewing excitement.

U.S. 20 likewise presents a spectacular setting but at a whisked pace. Here, Black Butte and Mount Jefferson are the skyline royalty. Side trips to such places as the Hoodoo Ski area/Big Lake area, Suttle Lake, and Black Butte, and access to luxury resorts and campgrounds can sidetrack travelers.

A trip into the Camp Sherman–Metolius River area slows the pace and treats eyes to a breathtaking spring-fed river. The Metolius Wild and Scenic River captivates with its deep trenches, riffles, and pools, and its ponderosa pine–western larch setting. Cedars grow riverside, and grassy bars and islands flaunt big-leaf lupine, Indian paintbrush, and monkey flower. This river secludes large wild trout, and its fly-fishing is world renowned. USFS campgrounds dot the recreation corridor, along with private campgrounds and resorts. Key attractions include the Head of the Metolius, the Camp Sherman fish-viewing platform, and Wizard Falls Fish Hatchery. Foot trails trace the river's banks.

Into the Forest
Robert Aufderheide Memorial Drive

Route 12

This 60-mile drive through Willamette National Forest follows Forest Road 19 between Westfir (west of Oakridge off Oregon Highway 58) and Blue River Junction (on Oregon Highway 126). Snow closes the route November to April.

Some backroad drives are about the big wow, while others are about the quiet seduction. Aufderheide Memorial Drive falls into the latter category. Named for a forest superintendent, this sojourn captivates with rich old-growth and mature forest, crystalline waters, access to trails, and freedom from the bustle beyond its insular woods. One of the first fifty routes recognized under the USFS National Scenic Byways system in 1988, this drive grew out of a horse and wagon trail from the late 1800s.

The byway travels along the North Fork of the Middle Fork Willamette River; Roaring River; and the South Fork McKenzie River and its impound, Cougar Reservoir. USFS campgrounds invite overnight stays. In June, rhododendron and dogwood blooms decorate the low-elevation Cascade forest.

Northbound, the drive begins in the one-time timber-mill town of Westfir, where tiny, well-kept former company cottages shape a quaint neighborhood. The drive starts at the 180-foot red span of Office Bridge, which once led to the mill office. Office Bridge is the longest covered bridge in Oregon. Its soaring roadway arch accommodated the loaded logging trucks; the adjoining covered foot walk allowed pedestrians to cross. A kiosk introduces the bridge and area history. Beneath the span flows the North Fork of the Middle Fork Willamette, a designated U.S. Wild and Scenic River.

A burgeoning trail will one day parallel the entire North Fork; segments are already in place at Westfir and places up canyon. Side roads lead to trailheads, while side-road bridges offer river overlooks. Although the backroad's draping maples, cedars, and firs can obstruct river viewing, they knit a soothing travel aisle. Where the river has carved out a gorge, the chunky basalt walls recall volcanic activity some 3 million years ago.

Constitution Grove (roughly midway along the route) provides a shadowy stroll through history in its pocket old-growth grove. The trees here were young when the United States was young, prompting the USFS to dedicate this grove on the 200th anniversary of the Constitution's signing. The big Douglas firs and cedars are now paired with commemorative wooden plaques identifying the Constitution signers.

Along the South Fork McKenzie, the French Pete Trail enters another realm of old-growth trees and sparkling waters. The rescue of the trees was the successful outcome of a bitter environmental battle in the 1970s. Another stop for seeing the big trees is Delta Campground; its nature trail through Delta Old-growth Grove wanders among trees that are 200 to 650 years old. Trails into the uncut wilds of Waldo Lake and Three Sisters wildernesses continue the big-tree discovery.

At Box Canyon, the old guard station and Landis Cabin offer touchstones to the past. Such outposts were critical to managing forests in the days when communication and transportation systems were crude. Besides serving as a base for forest maintenance, these posts provided a front-row defense in emergencies—anything from fighting fires to chasing sheep. The Civilian Conservation Corps built Box Canyon Guard Station and improved the wagon road that preceded the memorial byway.

The tumbling, white Roaring River, with its untrammeled mossy banks, accompanies the fast roadway descent. It is quickly replaced by the South Fork McKenzie River. The South Fork is more accessible than the Roaring River, with riverside campgrounds, turnouts, and trailheads. Deep pools reflect outcrop cliffs and towering trees. Elsewhere, cascades speed the South Fork's journey to the main stem McKenzie.

Cougar Reservoir, which captures the South Fork waters, signals a change in tempo. Contained by the tallest rock-fill dam in Oregon, the 6-mile-long canyon reservoir hosts a lively crowd of boaters and swimmers, with anglers finding places as well. The forest and rock of the canyon create an attractive backdrop.

Perhaps the most popular reservoir-area attraction is Terwilliger Hot

OVERLEAF:
The Ray Atkeson Trail along Sparks Lake provides this view of South Sister. Ray Atkeson was Oregon's photographer laureate. South Sister is one of a string of volcanoes between northern California and British Columbia.

Springs (a fee site where clothing is optional). A short trail leads to the steamy springs, lagoon, and the stepped pools that link the two. The parking area quickly fills on weekends; painted vans from the 1960s congregate here.

The drive concludes at Oregon Highway 126, gateway to recreation on the main stem of the McKenzie River or an avenue west to Eugene.

ON THE EASTERN SLOPE
Cascade Lakes Scenic Byway

ROUTE 13

This 72-mile drive begins west off U.S. Highway 97 in Bend (exit 138), following Colorado Boulevard to Century Drive and the Cascade Lakes Scenic Byway. The byway ends at Oregon Highway 58. The route is variously signed Century Boulevard, Cascade Lakes Highway, or Forest Road 46. It is open in its entirety from June to October.

At the eastern foot of the Central Cascades, this engaging drive strings together numerous lakes and takes in Cascade volcano views. Scenic America, a national organization recognizing natural beauty, named this byway one of the nation's ten "most important scenic byways." The route loosely follows the historic paths of Native Americans, trappers, and explorers. Others who have passed this way include John C. Fremont and Kit Carson.

Besides the headlining peaks and lakes, the stunning Deschutes River, pine forests, meadows, and lava-flows grace the roadway. The vehicle dress code here seems to call for a canoe or a pair of skis.

Mount Bachelor (site of the popular ski resort), South Sister, Broken Top, Maiden Peak, and Diamond Peak pop up along the forested skyline. The lakes melt into wildflower meadows threaded by meandering streams. In early morning, deer browse these meadows, sometimes wrapped in an aura of mist. Ospreys and eagles soar across the skies.

Stands of ponderosa pine threaded with bitterbrush, manzanita, and sticky laurel initially frame the travel aisle; farther along, lodgepole pines and firs vary the forest appearance. The byway accesses trails, campgrounds, picnic areas, sno-parks, and historic sites. Trails lead to a vast assortment of lakes, wilderness retreats, and high peaks. Accommodations run from luxury resorts to rustic campgrounds.

Early in the trip, Meadow Picnic Area offers a charming first acquaintance with the Deschutes Wild and Scenic River. Acclaimed for its fishing and beauty, the Deschutes is the life thread flowing through this part of Oregon, feeding downstream ranches, fields, and cities. Whitewater rafters roar over the less tumultuous chutes that lend the river its name; other plummets are unnavigable, tumbling over old lava dams.

A bold view of South Sister precedes Sparks Lake, the first of the roadside lakes. Its expanse and puzzle-piece shape make the shallow lake difficult to fully appreciate from any one spot. The water sweeps away to yellow-spangled meadow, dark forest, and lava flow. Sparks Lake was a favorite of Oregon photographer laureate Ray Atkeson. A memorial trail in his honor briefly travels along the shore, arriving at a knock-out view of South Sister, Mount Bachelor, and their watery doubles. Treed islands and volcanic outcroppings contribute to the interesting stage, as does a lava chasm on the trail's interlocking loop.

Devils Garden, where a lava flow nudges the road, captures visitors' respect and imagination. Here, the jumbled rocks and crags shoot 200 feet skyward. Native American legend places at this site a clash between suitors over a Klamath Indian maiden. A few faint pictographs rest in the volcanic jumble, but the primary rock art fell victim to vandalism. In the mid 1960s, Apollo astronauts trained at central Oregon's lava flows; astronaut James Irwin carried a piece of the area's volcanic rock to the moon.

A 3-mile crescent spur visits Elk Lake, Hosmer Lake (popular for canoeing and fly-fishing), and the restored 1929 Elk Lake Guard Station. The classic log guard station serves as a seasonal visitor center. At Hosmer, waders and float tubes are standard gear, and Atlantic salmon offer a challenge to fly-anglers. Wind-billowed sails glide across Elk Lake, which provides views of Bachelor, Broken Top, and South Sister.

Farther south sit bigger lakes and reservoirs. Of these, Cultus and Wickiup serve water-skiers; all invite fishing; and many allow boats with trolling motors. Unlike much of the area, which is dressed in skinny, hardy lodgepole pines, Cultus Lake has a border of mature fir and ponderosa pine. Hikers visiting Cultus Lake will find a fine trail striking out for Three Sisters Wilderness. Wickiup, the largest body of water, was named for the frame poles of the wickiup structures left by the Native Americans who once fished and hunted here. The poles still stood at the time the lake was flooded in 1949.

Osprey Observation Point, on Crane Prairie Reservoir, looks out on an important breeding ground for the fish hawks. They nest atop drowned snags and soar across the Cascade Lakes' skyway from May through October. Davis Lake completes the roll call of lakes. Abutted by lava flow, this large natural lake fluctuates with the rainfall and sits under the watch of Maiden Peak.

Along the byway, side roads branch east to Sun River, La Pine, and U.S. 97, allowing drivers to shorten the trip or fashion a loop. At Crescent Creek Cut-off, travelers can loop back to Bend via U.S. 97 or complete the byway heading west to Highway 58.

Herders moved their sheep up and down the mountains between pastures. Hinton is shown with his sheep near South Sister in 1916. (Courtesy of the United States Forest Service)

PART III

THE SOUTHWEST:
JEFFERSON COUNTRY

FACING PAGE:

The explosion of Mount Mazama 7,700 years ago created the caldera basin in which Crater Lake eventually formed. This lake, rimmed by 2,000-foot cliffs, is one of the clearest lakes in the world, and is noted for its intense blue color.

ABOVE:

Wildflowers decorate this pasture near Broadbent on the Rogue-Coquille Scenic Byway.

In this region of great ecological, geographical, and cultural diversity, economies based on natural resources represent the common thread. This region encompasses the southern coast, the Siskiyou Mountains, the Umpqua and Rogue river valleys, their associated Cascade Mountain forests, and Klamath Basin. Major towns include Coos Bay, Bandon, Gold Beach, Brookings, Roseburg, Grants Pass, Medford, Ashland, and Klamath Falls.

Fish, gold, timber, fur, and productive land and water attracted settlement here, and working communities now dot the region. But as resources dwindle and values and policies change, these communities have had to grapple with their identities. Backing up their historical bases of fishing, lumbering, ranching, and farming is a new breed of enterprises: tourism, small businesses, medical services (in Medford), and retirement living. Although changes have kept larger towns viable, remote outposts still struggle.

A fierce independence and self-reliance characterizes southwest Oregon. The region's independent streak can be traced back to the 1941 attempt to secede from Oregon and unite with northern California as the breakaway state of Jefferson. While the borders never formed, the mindset did. Other pages in history tell of the Applegate Trail and the trial and execution of Captain Jack, the Modoc leader whose northern California standoff with the government sparked national attention. Gold strikes, reckless boomtowns, and Chinese miners enrich the archives.

Travelers find a varied landscape. Backdrops include stunning cliffs and beach shores, pastoral coastal valleys of cranberry bogs and dairy farms, and the botanically diverse Siskiyou Mountains, which possess one of the richest plant inventories in the nation. The river valleys sandwiched by the Siskiyous and Cascades enjoy a warm climate attractive to retirees and ideal for crops. Sheep and cows graze the oak-studded, grassy hillsides, as do deer and elk.

In the Cascades, the upper Umpqua and Rogue rivers meander through bountiful national forests of big firs. In the eastern rain shadow stretches the Klamath Basin, with its massive lakes and farms of barley, oats, and potatoes. The lakes and associated wetlands form a critical migratory stopover on the Pacific Flyway. Winter marks the gathering of the largest concentration of bald eagles outside of Alaska. Besides all that, Jefferson Country is home to Oregon's lone national park, Crater Lake.

From professional-level golf at Bandon to Shakespeare productions in Ashland to jet boat rides on the Rogue River, this region covers a wide spectrum of leisure pursuits. The Umpqua River offers world-class fly-fishing, and birding in the Klamath Basin ranks among the finest in the nation. Rafting, canoeing, boating, and hiking capture avid followings.

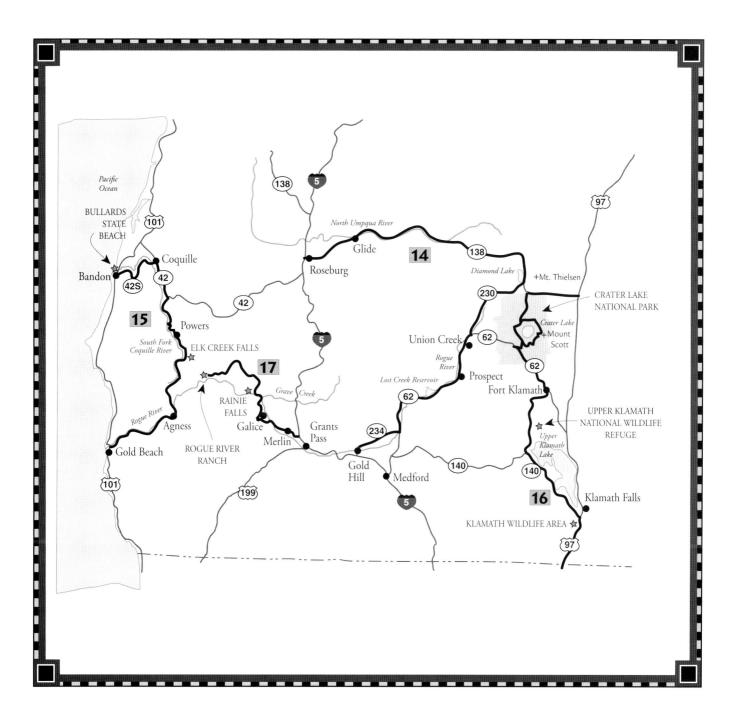

Pacific
Ocean

BULLARDS
STATE
BEACH

101

Coquille

42

15

42S

Bandon

Powers

South Fork
Coquille River

ELK CREEK FALLS

17

RAINIE
FALLS

Galice

Agness

ROGUE RIVER
RANCH

Rogue River

Merlin

Gold Beach

101

199

138

5

North Umpqua River

Glide

Roseburg

14

138

Diamond Lake

+Mt. Thielsen

97

230

CRATER LAKE
NATIONAL PARK

Crater Lake

+Mount
Scott

Union Creek

62

Rogue
River

Lost Creek Reservoir

Prospect

62

Fort Klamath

62

UPPER KLAMATH
NATIONAL WILDLIFE
REFUGE

Upper
Klamath
Lake

5

Grave Creek

Grants
Pass

234

62

Gold
Hill

Medford

140

140

5

16

Klamath Falls

KLAMATH WILDLIFE AREA

97

RIGHT:

A fly fisher takes one last cast on Diamond Lake at sunset. The Rogue-Umpqua Scenic Byway provides anglers ample opportunity to try their luck.

BELOW:

Lost Creek Reservoir is a popular fishing and boating destination along the Upper Rogue River. Peyton Bridge spans the lake.

Segmented Clearwater Falls spills 30 feet and is one of several waterfalls easily accessed off the Rogue-Umpqua Scenic Byway. A rustic U.S. Forest Service campground and picnic area sits adjacent to the falls.

DRIVING RIVERS
Rogue-Umpqua Scenic Byway

This 165-mile byway loops east off Interstate 5 between Roseburg (exit 124) and Gold Hill (exit 40), following Oregon Highways 138, 230, 62, and 234.

Passing from oak-and-grass hills into rich fir forest, this route pursues two of Oregon's premier wild and scenic rivers, the North Umpqua and the Rogue. Other features of the drive are stunning waterfalls, mountain lakes, and volcano views. Outstanding trails, including the two national recreation trails that parallel the rivers, engage hikers. Frequent stopping is inevitable. For overnight stays, travelers will find ample public campgrounds, rustic lodges and cabins, and a historic hotel in Prospect.

Beginning in the timber town of Roseburg, the drive weaves through picturesque valley foothills and past a riverside county park to pursue the forested, aqua-green waters of the North Umpqua River upstream. At Glide, Colliding Waters bids a stop with its viewpoint, historic ranger station, and Native American history. Here, in spring runoff, the Little River crashes into the North Umpqua River in spectacular fashion. A Native American presence at the colliding waters can be traced back 5,000 years. The area provided the natives with salmon, berries, roots, and nuts, as well as plant fibers for weaving, and cobbles for making bowls. Plank housing saw them through the winter. The ranger station, a Civilian Conservation Corps project, is on the National Register of Historic Places.

The lower part of the river is open to all anglers, with the 31 miles above Deadline Falls restricted to fly-fishing only. The river's steelhead sport is world-renown, with 30-pound fish lifted from the river. Enthusiasts can book fishing-guide services. From May through October, salmon and steelhead jump the falls at Swiftwater County Park (site of Deadline Falls), Susan Creek Recreation Site, and Steamboat Falls.

The county park marks the western terminus to the 79-mile North Umpqua National Recreation Trail. A dozen primary trailheads dispersed along the drive allow hikers to break the trail into day-hike lengths.

Oregon Highway 138 pairs closely with the North Umpqua, allowing for frequent views of the scenic, winding river with its riffles, pools, and basalt outcrops. Skyline features of Eagle, Rattlesnake, and Old Man Rocks pierce the forest. Where ashy cliffs appear, visitors are looking at the ashfall from Mount Mazama, the ancient volcano that erupted and collapsed 7,700 years ago, ultimately creating Crater Lake.

After veering away from the North Umpqua, the drive passes a trio of roadside waterfalls: Watson, Whitehorse, and Clearwater. The 0.5-mile crescent trail at Watson Falls leads to three viewpoints for admiring the spiraling droplets of this 272-foot falls, which spills like gentle rain. Whitehorse Falls is a charmer, cupped in an old-growth amphitheater, and 30-foot Clearwater Falls has been the site of weddings.

About midway into the drive, Diamond Lake Recreation Area entices drivers aside. The destination encompasses the popular natural lake, a metropolis of shoreline campgrounds, and the accesses to lake, forest, and volcano trails. Pointy-topped Mount Thielsen and rounded Mount Bailey watch over the 3,000-acre lake, and a paved lakeshore trail provides up-close views. Depending on the time of year, visitors to the recreation area can enjoy boating, fishing, hiking, horseback riding, bicycling, snowmobiling, snowshoeing, and cross-country skiing. A shoreline resort rents boats and sports equipment.

Born on Union Peak at the outskirts of Crater Lake, the legendary Rogue River is a shimmering ribbon of uncommon beauty. Recreation spans its entire length to the sea. Crater Rim Viewpoint, on Highway 230, marks the start of the Upper Rogue National Recreation Trail. This trail parallels more than 40 miles of pristine river. It passes through lodgepole pine and old-growth forests, steep-walled pumiceous canyons, untrammeled meadows, and scoured basalt channels. Cascades, waterfalls, sterling tributaries, turbulent gorges, and vanishing waters are some of the river's attributes that can be seen from the national recreation trail or the road.

On Highway 62, at the confluence of Union Creek and the Upper Rogue River, sits the tiny historic community of Union Creek, with its rustic cabin resort. It is a site of big-tree majesty year round and dogwood blooms in May. Side trips lead to the Rogue Gorge Viewpoint and to Natural Bridge, where the whole river passes through a 200-foot-long lava tube. Native Americans and settlers would cross the Rogue River atop the tube; a pedestrian bridge serves contemporary feet.

Prospect, only slightly larger than Union Creek, marks the next brush with civilization. Its offerings include a ranger station, the historic Prospect Hotel, and a gateway to Mill Creek Falls Scenic Area. The hotel exudes bygone charm, from its wicker seating on the front porch to its elegant vintage dining room to its wispy lace curtains. At the scenic area, 173-foot Mill Creek Falls and equally tall Barr Creek Falls spill into the Rogue River.

Scenic Peyton Bridge precedes the river impound, Lost Creek Reservoir, which is the site of Joseph H. Stewart State Park and Cole M. Rivers Fish Hatchery. Boating and fishing enliven the lake. Below the dam, Casey State Park offers day use of the river and bustles with rod-carrying folk during salmon runs. Across the river, treetops hold an osprey nest and a heron rookery. At the height of the salmon-fly hatch, merganser broods partake of the easy dining. When the insects take to the sky, the lacy-winged phenomenon conjures thoughts of Alfred Hitchcock.

Farther along, fly-tying shops, fishing and drift-boating guide services, and raft rentals, along with the larger service community of Shady Cove, answer travelers' needs. The scenery turns to valley oaks and rolling grasslands. At the junction with Highway 234, drivers may follow Highway 62 west another 5 miles to Eagle Point, with its historic but still operating Butte Creek Flour Mill. Oregon Highway 234 carries the drive to its end.

On Highway 234, the rural sights and smells of the Agate Desert engage the senses. Cascade Mountain views are exchanged for Siskiyou Mountain images. Occupying the immediate skyline are twin landmarks, Table

ABOVE:

Mount Thielsen, elevation 9,182 feet, is a skyline emblem of the Southern Cascades, easily recognizable by its pointy top. The Indian name for this peak was His-chok-wol-as.

FACING PAGE:

Lodgepole pines and meadow shores enfold 3,000-acre Diamond Lake, a year-round recreation playground.

Rocks. These upper and lower mesas, jointly held by The Nature Conservancy and BLM, rise 800 feet from the valley floor and possess a botanically rich ecosystem. Wildflowers dress the Tables from March through June.

In the 1850s, gold lured people into Rogue River country. The tiny town of Gold Hill, named for the site of an early gold discovery, caps the tour.

SISKIYOUS TO THE SEA
Rogue-Coquille Scenic Byway

ROUTE 15

This 111-mile route shapes an arc east off U.S. Highway 101 between Gold Beach and Bandon. From Gold Beach, it heads east on Jerry's Flat Road (Curry County 595), which becomes Forest Road 33. From Forest Road 33, Oregon Highways 242, 42, and 42S lead to Bandon. All but 12 miles is paved; winter snow can close upper parts of Forest Road 33.

This quiet journey follows the Lower Rogue River upstream, crossing over the coastal mountains above Agness to follow the South Fork and main stem Coquille River out to sea. Settings include the riparian woodlands along the rivers, the mixed forest of the Siskiyou Mountains, and the rural images of the Coquille River floodplain. Sites recall maritime, Native American, and early mining history. Towns encountered include Agness, Powers, Myrtle Point, and Coquille. Agness, population "small" according to the sign hanging over the general store, captivates with the simple ease of a bygone era.

Gold Beach (originally Ellensburg) derives its name from a brief pioneer interlude into the gold fray of the 1850s, when placer sluice boxes jammed the beaches. The true bonanza, though, was salmon. Robert D.

The Coquille waterfront bustled in 1899; at dock are the Wolverine, Favorite, *and* Hilhelmina. *(Courtesy of Salem Public Library)*

Hume operated a successful salmon fishery, hatchery, and cannery here from 1876 to 1908. The Rogue River fishery remained the productive backbone to the community until 1935, when logging took the forefront. The river economy today is driven by outstanding sport fishing, jet-boat tours, hiking, rafting, and camping.

A thick shoulder of trees can mask the river as the backroad makes its way upstream along the south shore of the Lower Rogue River. Port of Gold Beach and USFS campgrounds shape opportunities for a Rogue River acquaintance. Turkey and deer visit campsites, ospreys nest above the river, and otters sometimes play on shore. Some river bar approaches can be steep and rough.

Coquille Civilian Conservation Corpsmen work at felling a snag on a fire line in the 1930s. (Courtesy of the United States Forest Service)

The Lower Rogue is a beautiful, broad river with wide cobble bars, scenic outcrops and boulders, and a varied edge of madrone, myrtle, cedar, and fir. The river's descriptively named Massacre Rock recalls a page from the Rogue River Indian Wars. Here the Gold Beach Guard ambushed two canoes of Indians in 1856. An Indian village occupied the shore about 5 miles upstream from Gold Beach.

Although this river is one of the state's premier recreational draws, its distance from population centers keeps crowds down. The Schrader Old-Growth and Myrtle Tree trails, both off Forest Road 33, introduce two of the region's engaging habitats. The myrtle tree is a southern Oregon hallmark, with eucalyptus-scented leaves, lovely branches, and prized wood. Myrtlewood shops pop up all along the southern coast, and few Oregon homes go without a finely crafted myrtlewood bowl.

A sequence of three bridges spanning three stunning waters—the Illinois Wild and Scenic River, Costa Shasta Creek, and the Rogue Wild and Scenic River—precedes the Agness turnoff. Agness is gateway to the two banner trails along the Siskiyou stretch of the Rogue. Downstream stretches the 12.5-mile Lower Rogue Trail; upstream is the 40-plus-mile Rogue River National Recreation Trail. The latter departs from Big Bend, an aptly named place on the river, and heads toward Grave Creek Bridge. En route, it passes Zane Grey's cabin and two national historic sites: Rogue River Ranch and Whiskey Creek Cabin.

Jet boats are a popular way to see the Rogue River and its deep forested canyon; the tours originate out of Gold Beach. Rafting and hiking are other ways to see the river canyon.

The Mary D. Hume *began and ended her days in Gold Beach. Over a span of ninety-seven years, the modified Brigantine sailing ship served as a coastal freighter, Arctic whaling vessel, towboat, halibut boat, and tugboat. The relic now sits below the Rogue River Bridge.*

LEFT:

The lower river valleys are ideal for ranching. This ranch is located along the South Fork Coquille River drainage.

BELOW:

The Siskiyou Mountains represent one the nation's most botanically diverse realms, but this understory carpet unites the commonplace starflower, oxalis, and sword fern.

THE *MARY D. HUME*

The *Mary D. Hume*, an early sailing ship listed on the National Register of Historic Place, is moored at the Port of Gold Beach below Patterson Bridge (the Rogue River Bridge). It is a fitting resting place, since she began her days here, constructed in 1881. Today, she's an old boat, weathered, with an algae coating and spots of grass on her deck. Her portholes are vacant and a few seabirds use her as a perch.

No doubt this charming relic could pass along tales of high-sea adventures. During her ninety-seven years in commercial service, this Brigantine sailing ship, with auxiliary steam power, worked as a coastal freighter, Arctic whaling vessel, towboat, halibut boat, and tugboat. She holds the distinction of being the longest-used commercial vessel on the Pacific Coast. Retired in 1978, she sailed under her own power back to Gold Beach.

The small river-outpost of Agness extends a congenial welcome, with its general store, post office, library, lodging, and small museum (open summers). The museum holds a delightful mix of artifacts and finds from "Grandma's attic." The collection includes a fine Native American display, 4,000- to 8,000-year-old petroglyphs, local pioneer history, and the baseball bat of Hall of Famer Bobby Doerr; volunteers supply the local flavor. Nostalgia reigns at the town's annual country fair, complete with pie-baking and watermelon-eating contests and the ringing of well-tossed horseshoes.

From Agness, the route passes up and over the Siskiyou Mountains to Powers. Although this unpaved stretch may be quiet, it does receive regular use. With the climb, bigger trees give shade. Along the South Fork Coquille River drainage, USFS campgrounds invite pause. The South Fork flows clear, threading around boulders and collecting in pools.

Approximately midway into the trip, trails visit Elk Creek Falls and Big Tree. Elk Creek Falls is a tall, shimmering, two-segment waterfall adorned by mosses. Big Tree is a champion 219-foot-tall Port Orford cedar. Rural images then usher drivers into Powers, which holds a ranger station, basic services, and a pleasant park with camping and day-use facilities. At the north end of town sits the Pioneer House museum.

The official USFS drive stops at Highway 42. It finishes off with blended rural and forest images: rustic barns, a slash burner, general stores with sawblade art, a country church, treed slopes, and ponies deep in wildflowers. At Highway 42, drivers can opt to continue 29 miles to Bandon for the full 111-mile journey, or strike east to Interstate 5.

Opting for Bandon, drivers encounter a much faster pace along Highway 42. The chronicle of early day logging at Myrtle Point's Coos County Logging Museum or the summer melodramas at Coquille's Sawdust Theatre are two reasons to stop. The quieter country highway of Highway 42 South rolls through a pastoral setting along the Coquille River floodplain. But the thick green pastures dotted by sheep, llamas, and dairy cows bow to the coastal impressions of Bandon.

Bandon boasts an attractive port, an old-town shopping district, and a beautiful stretch of coastline accented by sea stacks. Bullards State Beach, just north of town, offers camping and an extensive day-use area. The photogenic Coquille River Lighthouse is the park's star attraction. A relatively new destination, Bandon Dunes Golf Resort, completes the coastal signoff.

FIRE AND FEATHERS
Volcanic Legacy Scenic Byway

This drive through the southern Cascades and Klamath Basin is a journey of fire and feathers. The route crosses ashy pine forest and climbs to encircle the caldera rim of the miraculously blue Crater Lake, before descending into the mosaic of forest, range, lake, and wetland that makes up Klamath Basin. Skyline views include Mount Thielsen, the remnant volcanic cones of ancient Mount Mazama, the caldera of Mountain Lakes Wilderness, and California's Mount Shasta. A pumice desert, fumaroles (the welded spires around vents of escaping gas), and cinder cones continue the fiery tale.

Klamath Basin hosts 80 percent of the migratory birds on the Pacific Flyway. Millions of waterfowl arrive in the fall, along with an entourage of bald eagles.

The legacy from Mount Mazama's eruption and collapse precedes the turnoff to Crater Lake National Park. The nutrient-lacking, ash and pumiceous soils sustain only the hardiest of trees—the lodgepole pine. As the route climbs, the forest fills out, adding other species. Side roads offer detours to trailheads and other attractions. Near the drive's start, dusty Forest Road 70 leads to Desert Forest Journeys, consisting of a trio of nature trails and a short drive, which together tell the story of a ponderosa-pine ecosystem and early logging.

The route arrives at Crater Lake National Park via the north entrance. At the caldera, it adds a circle, following the 33-mile Rim Drive, which serves up multiple overlooks of the 5-mile-wide, 1,900-foot-deep lake. The sky and the steep-sided golden cliffs of the caldera are reflected in the mesmerizing lake. Piercing the lake, the volcanic cone of Wizard Island rises 700 feet above the surface. The small, aptly named jagged-top island, Phantom Ship, cuts an eerie profile. Place names such as Devils Backbone, Pumice Castle, Danger Bay, and Sun Notch spark the imagination. Several turnouts have panels explaining the area's geology and relating the associated Native American legends.

Rim Drive also leads to trails. Paths strike up Watchman Peak and Mount Scott (both of which hold lookouts), or descend to Cleetwood Cove, which is the launch site for the park's boat tour and the sole lake access. The boat tour is a fee attraction. At Rim Village, visitors find the historic Crater Lake Lodge (built in 1915 and completely restored), Sinnott Memorial Viewpoint, and the trail to Garfield Peak (elevation 8,060 feet). Many hikers consider Garfield Peak to have the finest summit view in the park. The village attends to needs with food services, a picnic area, and a small visitor center.

Travelers may opt for a detour off Rim Drive to the Pinnacles. This 6-mile detour finds an impressive canyon array of fumaroles (peculiar

This 140-mile byway begins at Diamond Lake Junction, the interception of U.S. Highway 97 and Oregon Highway 138 (10 miles south of Chemult). It follows Oregon Highway 138, Crater Lake North Entrance Road (closed in winter), Rim Drive, Oregon Highway 62, Weed Road, Sevenmile Road, Westside Road, and Highway 140 to U.S. 97 South, before ending at the California border.

Wizard Island is one of two cinder cones in Crater Lake; the other is submerged. The lake's blue color, always intense, takes on different hues with the changes in season and the angle of the sun.

This weather-tortured whitebark pine overlooks Crater Lake. The cones of the tree attract Clark's nutcrackers, and gray jays often perch on the branches, chastising passing hikers.

A rusting piece of abandoned farm equipment rests among the deep grasses of Klamath Wildlife Area. This state refuge on the Klamath River hosts wintering waterfowl.

Yellow-headed blackbirds frequent the many marsh lands of the Klamath Basin.

A Civilian Conservation Corps youth scales a ponderosa pine to hang a telephone line in the 1930s. (Courtesy of the United States Forest Service)

spire-shaped vents). Trails wander the rim of the narrow canyon, offering changing perspectives. Along one trail, visitors will find the abandoned East Entrance. Where the primary drive leaves the park, the Godfrey Glen and Annie Falls areas offer a second opportunity to see similar geologic features.

The park averages 44 feet of snow per year, and the white stuff can linger into July. Wildflowers have a brief season; their fragile blooms pierce the ash and pumice, top mountains, and grace creeks and waterfalls. Sightings of big wildlife are rare, but the Clark's nutcrackers, ground squirrels, and chipmunks are entertaining. Additional park overlooks and picnic areas, as well as the park's Mazama Campground, line the route south.

History flavors the journey at the hamlet of Fort Klamath. The frontier fort here garrisoned the Oregon Volunteer Cavalry between 1863 and

1890. Here the trial and execution of Captain Jack marked the final chapter in the Modoc Indian Wars (1872–1873). The military had been ordered to round up the Modocs and place them on a reservation with the Klamath Indians—their historic enemies. But under Captain Jack, a ragtag band of fifty-two Modocs held off cavalry troops, who were superior in number, for five months in the harsh land of what is now Lava Beds National Monument in northern California. Surrender, though, was inevitable. Newspaper reports of the standoff fanned the attention of the nation.

Today at the fort, simple white markers identify the graves of Captain Jack and three other Modoc leaders. Although a gopher-started fire swept much of the Fort Klamath Historic Site Museum, the graves were spared, along with a jail and an old post office. A recreated guardhouse now holds the replacement museum.

After Fort Klamath, the route takes a couple of jigs to travel the western outskirts of the Upper Klamath Basin. Pastures, barbed wire, rustic corrals, distant farmhouses, aspens, cattails, and forested slopes paint the backdrop. Signs announce side routes to trails entering the Sky Lakes and Mountain Lakes wildernesses.

By Crystal Springs Picnic Area, the route begins to edge Upper Klamath National Wildlife Refuge and its 90,000-acre lake. Boat launches at Malone Springs and Rocky Point offer easy access to the 9.5-mile Upper Klamath Canoe Trail. Rocky Point Resort rents canoes. The quiet paddle reveals marsh, open water, and forests, and offers chance encounters with beavers, geese, swans, and other wildlife. Primitive Odessa Creek Campground, off Highway 140, signals another chance to slide the canoe into refuge waters.

MOUNT MAZAMA

Scientists estimate that ancient Mount Mazama stood 12,000 feet high before its eruptive episode and collapse 7,700 years ago. The resulting basin (caldera) captured centuries of snowmelt and rainwater to give birth to Crater Lake. At 1,943 feet deep, Crater Lake is the deepest lake in the United States and one of the four clearest lakes in the world (Oregon's Waldo Lake, Lake Tahoe in the Sierra Nevada, and Lake Baikal in Siberia are the other three).

The Mazama eruption was forty-two times greater than the 1980 eruption of Mount Saint Helens, and it spewed forth 150 times more ash. A 6-inch blanket of ash fell across eight states and three Canadian provinces (5,000 square miles). The ash in Crater Lake National Park's Pumice Desert is 50 feet deep. Besides ash, torrents of gas-charged pumice and molten rock sped down the flanks of Mazama at upwards of 100 miles per hour. The resulting deposits hit temperatures of 750° Fahrenheit, and building gases escaped through vents. Around these vents, minerals welded into tall fumarole cones, which centuries of creek erosion have exposed to the world. Fumaroles can be seen in the Sand Creek canyon at The Pinnacles, and along the Annie Creek canyon at either Godfrey Glen or Annie falls.

Coastal fog frequently travels up the river canyons, including the Rogue River canyon, shown here.

Lupine finds habitat in many different terrains; this showcase of blooms decorates the floodplain of the Rogue River.

The remote Rogue River Ranch is a National Historic Place managed by the Bureau of Land Management. Reached via backroad, river raft, or trail, the grounds and buildings are open for touring. This two-story Main House was completed in 1903. At one time, the house was a store and center of the Billings Trade Company.

The drive now rolls over low, forested hills and dips back into the basin. From turnouts, travelers can view western grebes, herons, ducks, and terns. The view at Howard Bay provides the first sense of the enormity of Upper Klamath Lake.

Where U.S. 97 makes its quick run to the Oregon border, travelers can detour west on Miller Island Road to the Klamath Wildlife Area for birding. In spring, sandhill cranes can be seen with their young, and white pelicans adorn the sky. Owls favor the big shade trees near the old farm within the wildlife area. Views stretch across the marsh to Mount Shasta.

At the Oregon border, travelers may choose to end the drive, or follow U.S. 97 into California and extend this tour of fire and feathers to Lower Klamath National Wildlife Refuge.

ROGUE JOURNEY
Galice-Hellgate and Grave Creek to Marial National Back Country Byways

ROUTE 17

From Interstate 5, exit 61, travel begins along Merlin Road west and north to Merlin. Merlin-Galice Road then takes the tour to Galice and Grave Creek, where BLM routes 34-8-1, 32-7-19.3, 32-8-31, and 32-9-14.2 travel to Marial and the Rogue River Ranch National Historic Place (tour's end). The 56-mile combined route is paved and gravel; the second part is not for recreational vehicles and should be avoided in snow and heavy rain.

In the rugged isolation of the Siskiyou Mountains, this backroad combines two BLM back-country byways that follow the beautiful Rogue Wild and Scenic River. The Galice-Hellgate byway is a popular rafters' gateway to the Rogue, with shuttle services, lodging, rafting companies, and fishing guide services vying for business. The relative flurry of activity here amplifies the lonesomeness of the second byway from Grave Creek to Marial. The Marial leg climbs 3,000 feet skyward before dipping 3,000 feet back to the river; it travels along the edge of the Wild Rogue Wilderness. The byway corridor itself is wild enough for sightings of bear, deer, and wild turkey.

Once past the service community of Merlin, the byway is framed by dry slopes of pine, oak, and madrone, and grassy slopes dotted with firs. Interrupting these hillsides are sharply rising cliffs and outcrops. Where the roadway is cut into the hillside, vibrant Oregon sunshine, pale-yellow Siskiyou iris, and red Indian paintbrush provide color. Hellgate Canyon Viewpoint overlooks the stunning, deep, steep-sided river canyon and the downstream bridge.

Where the wiggly river and byway snuggle closer together, signed side roads (some rough) dip riverside to boat launches and picnic sites. Josephine County's Indian Mary Campground offers a comfortable park-like setting on the river; a second, more rustic county campground sits farther downstream. The river's riffles, bends, and straightaways captivate both river runner and byway traveler. Between the Hellgate Viewpoint and Galice, some forty named rapids excite the river, but until Grave Creek no rapid is bigger than a Class II.

Just before Galice, the Hellgate-Galice byway forks. The selected trip stays on the road ahead, following the river; the untaken left fork journeys west over the mountains to Agness and the coast. Galice offers a last chance for raft rentals and services.

The Rand Ranger Station/William B. Smullin Visitor Center (staffed from mid May through mid October) sits ahead. Here visitors can obtain brochures about the area, and the staff can advise them on road and river conditions. The ranger-station complex, built between 1933 and 1934 by the Rand Camp Civilian Conservation Corps, is recognized as a National Historic Place. During the Franklin D. Roosevelt years, the Rand Camp corps built roads, fought fires, and collected ticks for scientific study.

Grave Creek Bridge marks the start of the Grave Creek to Marial byway. Grave Creek is also the site of a popular river launch and two superb downstream trails. The 40-plus-mile Rogue River National Recreation Trail travels the north bank, and the 2-mile Rainie Falls Trail journeys along the south bank to the Class V Rainie Falls rapid and its associated river portage. Rainie Falls wears the name of the old salmon gaffer who kept a cabin at the base of the falls. Fish still can be seen leaping this 15-foot-high waterfall, which spans the breadth of the river.

BLM routes now carry the tour away from the Rogue. The byway's paved route keeps to the left, passing above the Grave Creek boat ramp. Its upward intent quickly puts drivers in touch with the steepness of the Siskiyou Mountains and the depth of the canyon. Turnouts reinforce the concept with breath-stealing views. The folds of the canyon frame picturesque scenes, and vultures soar on the canyon thermals.

About 3.5 miles into the climb, a left spur leads to Whiskey Creek Overlook. Drivers of larger vehicles should park along the byway and walk 0.1 mile to the view. A splendid panorama stretches downstream, with the serial Siskiyou ridges, textured forest, and conifer spires. Anyone who is poor with maps or prefers to avoid gravel stretches can turn around at the overlook. The overall wild impression it leaves shapes a fine finale.

For those who continue the drive, the silence grows strong. To avoid straying at junctions, drivers should check signs and consult maps. The byway passes through dry forest, big-fir settings, and areas where the trees have been harvested, now at different stages of regrowth. Views extend into the Rogue and Cow Creek drainages. Before the descent, the byway meets the paved Powers-to-Glendale Road. Used by bicyclists, this side route offers additional backroad discoveries and an alternate return to Interstate 5 (consult maps).

At Marial, byway travelers take the turn toward the river and the historic ranch. The spanking-white Rogue River Ranch, now a museum and a National Historic Place, was the social hub for this remote reach. Its various roles included boarding house, post office, dancehall, church, and trading post. Visitors can stroll the grounds, visit the ranch-complex buildings, or check out the river. The backtracking return to Merlin and Interstate 5 offers a new perspective.

PART IV

THE NORTHEAST:
COLUMBIA PLATEAU TO
WALLOWA HIGH COUNTRY

FACING PAGE:

The Lower Deschutes River twists through arid canyon en route to the Columbia River.

ABOVE:

Abandoned homesteads and ghost towns dot the eastern Oregon landscape and recall the struggles of early miners and ranchers.

The northeast region encompasses the broad arid steppes of the Columbia Plateau, the high mountain splendor of the Blue and Wallowa ranges, and the deepest gorge in North America—the Snake River Canyon (Hells Canyon), at the Oregon-Idaho border. It is a region of few people, few stoplights, and big landscapes.

The Columbia Plateau rolls out a thin-soiled open range of basalt terraces, sweeping wheat expanses, sagebrush scrub, and deep-carved drainages. The Deschutes, Umatilla, and John Day rivers push through to the Columbia River. The Oregon Trail cuts a swath of human history across the plateau. In the badlands of John Day Fossil Beds National Monument rests a rich fossil record, dating from 29 to 50 million years ago.

The understated Blue Mountains stand distinct from Oregon's other mountain ranges. Fashioning this range are long, rounded, bald ridges; sweeping meadows; forests of pine, fir, and larch; freestanding stone pillars; and the stunning crests of the Elkhorn and Strawberry mountains. The area holds some of the state's largest herds of deer and elk. The wet and dry meadows are colored by a kaleidoscope of blooms.

The Blue Mountains only opened up in 1858, when Oregon finally overturned the directive prohibiting settlement east of the Cascades. Gold discoveries brought the earliest settlers, with Baker City burgeoning as the "queen city" of commerce. Ghost towns, adits, ditches, tailings (mining rubble), and stamp-mill ruins are reminders of the era.

At the state's far northeastern corner sits the juxtaposition of the Wallowas and Hells Canyon—magnificent extremes. The Wallowas captivate travelers with high granite peaks and ridges, glacier-carved valleys, alpine forests and meadows, high lakes, and wild and scenic rivers. Hells Canyon National Recreation Area enfolds the deep-gouged canyons of the Snake and Imnaha rivers. Steep terrain, arid steppes, dry forest, and basalt terraces characterize the uncompromising wild. Each landscape wears the imprint of the Nez Perce Indians. The Wallowas were the traditional homeland; Hells Canyon is where the tribe made its miraculous fording of the unfettered Snake River in a desperate flight for freedom. In 1992, the Hells Canyon Preservation Committee and the National Parks Conservation Association proposed that the Wallowas and Hells Canyon be designated a national park area called Hells Canyon National Park and Preserve. Legislation remains before Congress.

The small-town economies in this region are primarily based in logging, ranching, and farming. Tourism puts on a strong face in places like Baker City and Joseph. The town of Joseph features a magnificent outdoor gallery of life-size bronze sculptures. The isolation of the region produces, or perhaps attracts, the self-sufficient, but travelers will find the people friendly and helpful. Longtime residents have strong generational ties to the region; newcomers quickly forge a protective tie.

Rafting, fishing, hiking, horseback riding, wildlife viewing, history tracking, and self-discovery are northeast-region pursuits.

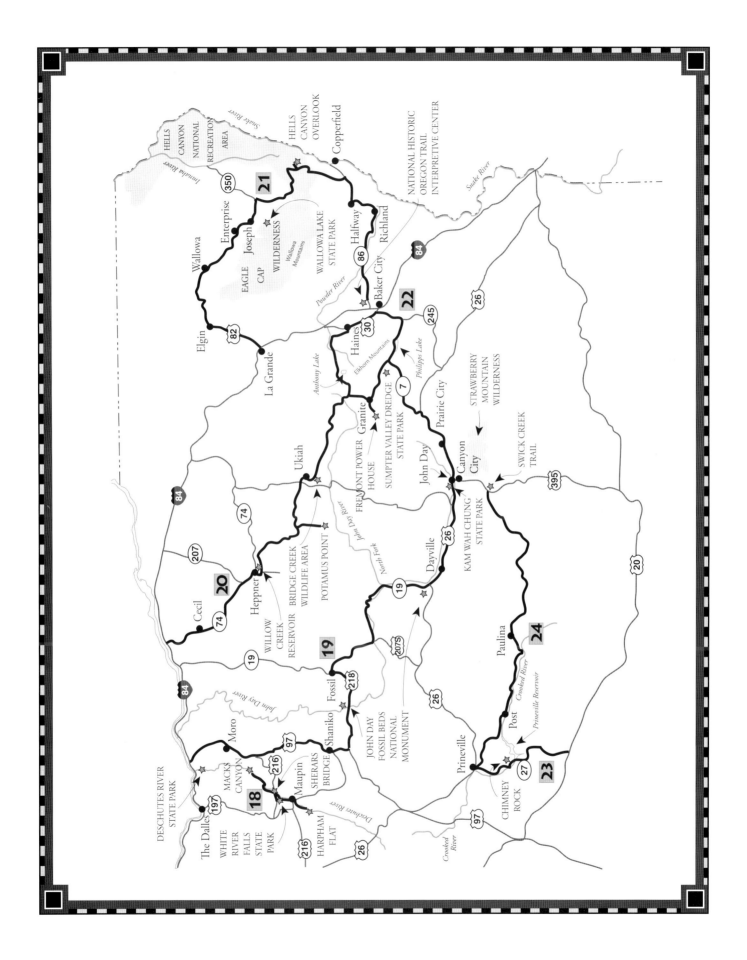

The shade tree beside this shack stands in contrast to the sagebrush-grassland expanse of the open high desert.

LEFT:
The Deschutes Wild and Scenic River is popular for rafting, drift boating, and world-class fishing. Bureau of Land Management campgrounds line the lower river.

FACING PAGE, TOP:
On the Deschutes River, Maupin is the area center for fly-tying shops, rafting companies, and shuttles.

FACING PAGE, BOTTOM:
Steelhead and trout try the wiles of Deschutes River anglers. The golden grasses of the river canyon cast a yellow glow across the water.

CHUTES AND FLY-LINES
Lower Deschutes River National Back Country Byway

Maupin (midway between The Dalles and Madras on U.S. Highway 197) provides access to this linear drive that follows the east bank of the Deschutes River from the gate 7.5 miles upstream from town to Macks Canyon, 26 miles downstream from town. Parts of the road are all-weather gravel. A 4-mile spur to White River Falls on Oregon Highway 216 can be added.

Disturbed by rapids and teeming with native redsides (redband rainbow trout), steelhead, and salmon, the Deschutes Wild and Scenic River rolls out an exciting canvas. The river and its closely paired byway twist through a dramatic high-desert canyon with exceptional scenery. BLM and city recreation sites provide river access, as well as camping and day-use facilities. Maupin's many float-trip operators, fishing-guide services, and fly-tying shops speak to the recreational aspect of the river.

Maupin bears the name of the pioneer family who started the first ferry here in 1872, but the town didn't really come into being until after 1911, a year that marked the great railroad race to serve Central Oregon. Competing tracks stretched along both banks of the Deschutes, and homesteaders followed the railroad. Although the west-bank line remains active, the byway and a downstream recreational trail have reclaimed the east-bank line.

Mergansers, Canada geese, kingfishers, vultures, ospreys, and hawks animate the water and sky of the river corridor. Swifts and swallows pour from the towering cliffs. Travelers can see deer at the river's edge or otters rolling and playing in the water. During the morning and evening hours, beaver wakes can cut the golden glow on the water. Because rattlesnakes and poison oak also find habitat here, travelers should be alert while exploring on foot.

The cliff palisades and columnar basalts formed 11 million years ago. The higher remote reaches of the canyon provide habitat for bighorn sheep, reintroduced in 1993. Area petroglyphs provide evidence of a once-native bighorn herd. Hackberry, sumac, juniper, ponderosa pine, and alder dot the otherwise arid stage. Wildflowers bring a parade of color—yellows, fuchsias, whites, and lavenders—from spring through fall.

Upstream from Maupin, the byway bears west off U.S. 197. Rafter launches and quiet fishing spots isolated by steep banks attract their respective followings, while the stunning vertical canyon and picturesque river attract sightseers. At Boxcar Rapids, road travelers can watch river runners attack the Class III rapids. Some thirty rapids trouble the river between the Harpham Flat boat launch and the unnavigable Class VI Sherars Falls downstream. After Harpham Flat, the road suffers from washboard stretches and potholes.

The byway segment downstream from Maupin leads to more stunning landscapes, chance wildlife sightings, and places to pause riverside. Beautiful bends, straightaways, trenches, riffles, and glassy stills characterize the river. Fly-lines dance over the water's surface; drift boats and rafts can be seen. Travelers can watch river runners at the Surf City and Oak Springs Rapids, about 4 miles north of town.

For thousands of years, Native Americans fished these waters. During adequate fish runs, members of the Confederated Tribes of Warm

Springs take part in traditional dip-net fishing. But, whether in use or not, the rickety dipping platforms along Sherars Falls are always a marvel, as are the huge silvery fish that jump into the tumult.

Pioneer history also graces the area. After being mistakenly led across the high desert by mountain man Stephen Meek, the Lost Wagon Train of 1845 made a desperate Deschutes River crossing near Sherars Falls. The first bridge crossing here, part of an 1860s military wagon road, was used by the Pony Express.

At Oregon Highway 216, drivers have the option of detouring west to White River State Park. Here, in its urgency to join the Deschutes River, the White River spills in a staircase trio of waterfalls. The upper two waterfalls plummet 140 feet. The falls can be viewed from the park overlook and a canyon trail, which also passes the ruins of a 1900s power plant.

Remaining on the byway, the route briefly jogs right on Highway 216 before resuming downstream over dusty gravel road. Lichen-painted rims, steep dusky slopes, and scree skirts contribute to canyon impressions. Downstream from Beavertail Recreation Site sits an island clad in incense cedar—a rarity, both at this elevation and east of the Cascades.

Macks Canyon Recreation Site marks the road's end. The fenced area here encloses the historic site of a Native American pit-house village dating back 2,000 years. Historically, such villages dotted the river, as the Native Americans would stay the winter, catching and drying fish. This site was excavated in the late 1960s.

The return backtracks to Highway 216, U.S. 197, or Maupin.

Above Sherars Falls on the Lower Deschutes River sat Sherars Hotel. This is how it looked in 1918. (Courtesy of Crook County Historical Society)

Picturesque Strawberry Lake in the Strawberry Mountain Wilderness is a popular spot for campers, hikers, and equestrians.

LEFT:

Fencelines are part of the western frontier; this line runs through the tall grass of the John Day River valley.

ABOVE:

Lichen-etched, weather-beaten barns and outbuildings pepper backroad views. This one is located near Austin Junction.

LEFT:

A leaf fossil marks the rock along the Trail of the Fossils at the Clarno Unit of John Day Fossil Beds National Monument. This badland countryside secludes fossils dating back 50 million years.

JOHN DAY COUNTRY
Journey Through Time Scenic Byway

ROUTE 19

This 276-mile byway offers a quiet alternative to Interstate 84 between Biggs (exit 104) and Baker City. It follows, in turn, U.S. Highway 97, Oregon Highway 218, Oregon Highway 19, U.S. 26, and Oregon Highway 7.

A celebration of the western frontier and a travelogue through time, this drive offers a chance to walk among 40-million-year-old mammalian fossils, cross swords with the Oregon Trail, wander with ghosts in forgotten towns, or get swept up in a cattle drive. The rollercoaster route crosses the wheat lands and sagebrush scrub of the Columbia Plateau, the ash-clay badlands and irrigated fields of the Lower John Day River Valley, the ranchland of the upper valley, and the rolling forests of the Blue Mountains. Small agricultural, ranch, and logging communities, many with small museums, dot the way. Recreation sites offer picnicking, John Day River access, or camping.

From Biggs, the byway twists south through arid Spanish Hollow, following the course of an 1869 military wagon road. Ideally suited to wheat, a fine wind-deposited, ice-age soil blankets the rolling terraces. The Columbia Plateau is one big kiss of land and sky. Emphasizing the vacant expanse are isolated barns, a solitary windmill, or the endless ranks of power lines.

Shaniko, a ghost town that has shaken off the cobwebs, invites travelers into the past. This town blossomed into being when it was selected as a terminus for the Columbia Southern Railroad. Following the rail here were inland freight and stage services to the newly opened lands east of

Before the success of motor vehicles, horses and liveries, such as the Dickson Livery Stable, shown here in 1900, were critical to a town's prosperity. (Courtesy of Crook County Historical Society)

the Cascades. The town grew to be the nation's largest wool shipping center. Its thirteen saloons hosted their share of fights, and story has it that the last range war took place here. Perhaps fittingly, it was the railroad's closure in 1911 that signaled the town's bust.

The town has a mix of rustic vacant buildings and those spruced up for company. In the freshly painted pastel shops, visitors find antique stores, trading posts, and old-time photography. The fully restored Shaniko Hotel exudes bygone elegance; the shady veranda seems designed for watching the day creep by. A jail wagon, schoolhouse, church, and city hall also offer views back in time.

Past Antelope, the route enters the Lower John Day River Valley. This major river flows 318 miles from its origin in the Blue and Strawberry mountains to its mouth on the Columbia River. The river is famous for its fishing and rafting. The lands it irrigates add a shock of green to the setting of arid dusky terraces and dark basalt rims.

John Day was a Pacific Fur Company hunter who met with misfortune on the Mau Hau River (now the John Day River). The hunter also lends his name to a town and the 14,000-acre John Day Fossil Beds National Monument. Two of the three monument units sit along the byway; the third, Painted Hills, is reached via a lengthy but worthwhile detour.

The monument's Clarno Unit introduces colorful palisades of eroded ancient mudslides, while the Sheep Rock Unit holds volcanic ash beds slowly giving up secrets millions of years old. Short interpretive trails enter each realm. At the Sheep Rock Unit, visitors will find the monument's Thomas Condon Visitor and Paleontology Center (the fossil museum) and historic Cant Ranch (the cultural museum). This unit also holds architectural Cathedral Rock, which overlooks the byway. The 500-foot vertical walls of Picture Gorge frame the drive's departure from Sheep Rock Unit.

Drivers wanting to see the third unit of the national monument may opt to detour south on Highway 207 at Service Creek or west on U.S. 26 from its junction with Highway 19, near the Sheep Rock Unit. The painted hills sit northwest of Mitchell off U.S. 26. Rain can emphasize the banding of red, gold, and black, but the colorful hills always enchant onlookers and inspire photographers.

Although fossil collecting is prohibited within the monument, the tiny town of Fossil (where Highway 19 picks up the tour) allows digging at a bed adjacent to the town high school. This fossil bed was revealed

ABOVE, TOP:

Logging has been an economic thrust in many Oregon towns. Here, workers at the Fred Carlen Sawmill in Canyon Creek pose for photos in 1910. Moving thick old-growth logs required teams of horses. (Courtesy of Grant County Historical Museum)

ABOVE, BOTTOM:

The Blue Mountains were populated with gold miners in the late 1800s. Waterwheels commonly powered the stamp mills that processed the ore. This is the waterwheel at the Dixie Creek Stamp Mill, in 1895. (Courtesy of Grant County Historical Museum)

When touring the Journey Through Time route, barns of unique character and size call photographers to their art. Much of the John Day Country is ranching territory.

Fire engines were critical to the health of wood-constructed early-day towns, such as Shaniko. This ghost town is percolating with new life as travelers try to capture the magic of a bygone era. Relics of history are at every turn.

The Kam Wah Chung & Company Museum in John Day is a time capsule that reveals the history of the Chinese in eastern Oregon. At the pharmacy, Doc Hay dispensed powders and herbs to heal patients of both Chinese and Caucasian ancestry.

The historic Shaniko Hotel, a charming landmark in the town of Shaniko, is still open for business.

Pioneer cemeteries recall both existing and deserted communities; this cemetery sits near Moro, Oregon.

KAM WAH CHUNG & COMPANY MUSEUM

In John Day sits this remarkable time capsule, listed on the National Register of Historic Places. Within its doors is the history of Chinese immigrants in early eastern Oregon. The building, a trading post on The Dalles Military Road, was purchased in 1887 by two industrious immigrants, "Doc" Ing Hay and Lung On. They were among the hundreds of Chinese who came to the West because of work in the gold fields or on the railroads. An 1879 census for eastern Oregon shows a population of 2,468 Chinese and 960 whites.

Serving both the white and Chinese populations, Doc Hay was a respected pulsologist (a diagnostician who analyzes pulses) and herbalist; Lung On was a merchant. Both won relative acceptance from the white community and could mediate on behalf of the Chinese miners. The building served as a store, pharmacy, bank, temple, meeting place, and home. The local Chinese workers would gather here to worship, gamble, and smoke opium. With the death of Doc Hay in 1948, the doors closed and nothing was disturbed until the museum opened in 1978.

Within the untouched collection are more than 500 herbs, bootleg whiskey, fireworks, canned goods, religious artifacts, business papers, and more. The windowless, reinforced barricade of the store indicates that while the two won respectability, they still could face drunken gunplay or torment from the area cowboys.

Guided tours introduce the time period and the collection of artifacts. The museum is open May through October; visitors should call for hours.

during school construction in 1949. Part of the Bridge Creek Flora formation, the fossil plant deposit here is between 1 and 32 million years old. Fossils of leaves, ferns, seeds, and nuts can be carefully removed from the hillside.

The tri-town area of John Day, Canyon City, and Prairie City shape the core service area for the route and the surrounding ranch communities. The trio also provides access to the Strawberry Mountain Wilderness, with its hiking, fishing, and horseback riding. All three towns trace their origins to gold, but ranching and logging are mainstays. Seasonally, ranchers still drive their cattle through the town at John Day. Museums in each town introduce pages of regional history. The Kam Wah Chung & Company Museum in John Day recognizes the influence and role of Chinese immigrants here.

Twisting forest travel characterizes the final part of the journey, with the road pulling up from the juniper-grass hills into the quiet, conifer-clad slopes of the Blue Mountains. Meadow openings can expose deer, elk, sandhill cranes, and coyotes. Vistas and brushes with history unfold with the miles.

From where the byway meets Elkhorn Scenic Byway (see route 22, "Ghosts of Gold"), it's a 26-mile drive east on Highway 7 to Baker City and Interstate 84.

SINGING THE BLUES
Blue Mountain Scenic Byway

This quiet byway travels a lightly inhabited reach of the state. From the Columbia Plateau scrubland, the route traverses the rolling wheat fields and irrigated pastures of the Willow Creek drainage before entering the Blue Mountain forests and prairie meadows. The tour ends at the North Fork John Day Wild and Scenic River, meeting the Elkhorn Scenic Byway (see route 22, "Ghosts of Gold"). Deer, elk, and antelope favor the Blue Mountain remoteness. Bridge Creek Wildlife Area, an extensive prairie basin, offers a good chance at spying Rocky Mountain elk. The towns of Heppner (population 1,400) and Ukiah (population 250) provide primary services. Picnic spots, campgrounds, lakes, trails, and overlooks suggest stops.

Sheep ranching played an early role in the settlement of Willow Creek Valley and continues to have a presence, along with wheat farming and cattle raising. At historic Cecil, now a private ranch, an old sheepherder's wagon and a "sheep dog crossing" sign reflect that legacy, but from May 15 to November 15, the woollies are off to summer pastures. Cecil marks where the Oregon Trail left what is now Morrow County, heading west. The one-time community traces its beginning to Oregon Trail pioneer William Cecil, who stopped here to repair his wagon and was quickly employed in the repair of the wagons belonging to fellow pioneers. The family stayed on. The first store and post office, built in 1867, are visible west of the byway, on private property where trespassing is prohibited.

Willow Creek is a deep-cut drainage with a light flow, because of irrigation, and only a few willows. But in June 1903, the creek put on a different show, when a sudden electrical storm and cloud burst unleashed a raging torrent. The onslaught swept up trees and buildings, destroying much of Main Street in the town of Heppner and taking 247 lives. It remains one of the worst flood disasters in the nation. Today, a dam above Heppner keeps the river quiet.

Heppner is an idyllic, fresh-faced little agricultural town, complete with a frequently photographed historic courthouse and a tree-shaded park. The Morrow County Museum and the Agricultural Collections Museum portray pioneer life. Murals on the latter's building depict the history of farming in the region.

Off Highway 207, at the south end of Heppner, Willow Creek Road, which later becomes Forest Road 53, takes the journey east. It follows Willow Creek upstream to the dam and its impound and then into the Blue Mountains. Although the purpose of the dam was to control flooding and provide irrigation, the resulting sun-drenched, 125-acre lake also serves recreation, with camping and boating facilities, and bass and trout fishing. Farther up canyon, in forest, Cutsforth County Park offers family camping facilities and has a fish pond ideally suited for children.

Side roads branch to trailheads, Pentland Lake (5 miles off into the

From Interstate 84, exit 147, this 130-mile paved backroad follows Oregon Highway 74, Oregon Highway 207 South, Willow Creek Road/Forest Road 53, Highway 244, and Forest Road 52, ending at Elkhorn Scenic Byway, near Granite. It is generally open June 15 to October 15.

Isolated homesteads dot the Columbia Plateau. The thin soils of the plateau produce quantities of wheat.

RIGHT:
Barbed wire is a ranching staple; this lassoed corral post stands near Well Spring.

At nearly 122,000 acres in size, the North Fork John Day Wilderness encompasses the North Fork John Day Wild and Scenic River, the telltale signs of pre-wilderness mining, and a legacy of forest growth and fire. A trail open to hikers and equestrians parallels the river, cutting into the wilderness.

A 39-mile segment of the North Fork John Day River is designated as a national wild and scenic river. Early placer mining has left a legacy of piled cobbles along the river plain.

forest) or Ditch Creek Guard Station (available for overnight rental). The Umatilla National Forest map can help travelers sort out options. During this relaxing meander, forest, wildfire-caused burns, dispersed aspens, scenic meadows, and a dusting of wildflowers contribute to windshield viewing.

About 76 miles into the drive, a 16-mile detour on gravel Forest Roads 5327 and 5316 leads to Potamus Point, a geologic overlook of the 2,000-foot canyon drop-off to Potamus Creek. An interpretive board titled "Floods of Fire" sits above the left side of Forest Road 5316 and marks the overlook. Drivers should watch for the sign, because it can be easily missed, and the road continues. Part of the Picture Gorge Basalt, the canyon has plummeting sides, steppe forest, and basalt terraces. The fourteen visible basalt layers were laid in separate volcanic episodes, spaced over thousands of years, during which the earth pulled apart and oozed lava. Millions of years of erosion by Potamus Creek then sliced into this geologic layer cake, revealing the history.

Byway travel resumes east on Forest Road 53 to Highway 244 and the Ukiah Valley. Picturesque Camas Creek nurtures this valley. Native Americans would gather here in early summer when the blue camas bloomed; the bulb was a primary food. Ukiah, a cute frontier town of logs and antlers, offers services. At the town park, the byway turns south toward Granite.

Four miles south of Ukiah, the route (Forest Road 52) edges Bridge Creek Wildlife Area. A primitive road enters the property, an area of sweeping prairie with enclaves of ponderosa pine. Spread over 13,000 acres, the wildlife area shapes an open space and critical winter habitat for Rocky Mountain elk and other large mammals. Another mile farther on Forest Road 52 is the turnoff for a USFS interpretive site and trail. The short trail leads to a rim overlooking Bridge Creek Wildlife Area and offers a chance to spy some of the thousand elk that pass the winter here. November through May is the best time for seeing the elk, but the elk hang around year round. Visits timed to early morning or late afternoon improve the odds of seeing elk. Coyotes, mule deer, and bald eagles also attract attention.

The drive resumes through forest and later offers an overlook of the North Fork John Day River Canyon. The route edges the river's wilderness before meeting the Elkhorn Scenic Byway at the North Fork John Day Campground and Trailhead. More otherworldly burns make a patchwork of the slopes. A beetle infestation here made the lodgepole pines vulnerable to fire; although it's destructive, fire is a natural process and ultimately benefits the forest.

The North Fork John Day Wild and Scenic River, its associated wilderness, and the byway crossroads make the North Fork John Day Campground an ideal base from which to explore. Day hikes along the river reveal the mining legacy: sagging cabins, mounded tailings, and rusting relics. Elkhorn Scenic Byway builds on the historical and forest portrait.

PARADISE FOUND
Hells Canyon Scenic Byway, Main Loop

ROUTE 21

This backroad revels in spectacle. It travels the ranchland of the Grande Ronde and Wallowa river valleys, passes around and through the Wallowa high-mountain grandeur, overlooks the stunning, harsh wild of Hells Canyon, and traverses Pine Creek Valley to meet up with the Oregon Trail at Flagstaff Hill. Welcoming small towns, the bronze art at Joseph, or a live production at the 1912 Elgin Opera House can waylay travelers. The heritage of the Nez Perce Indians lives on in the landmarks, the celebrations, and the spirit of the land.

For outdoor recreation, the region teems with opportunities: camping, hiking, horseback riding, rafting, and fishing. For trail information and passes, three USFS offices in La Grande, Enterprise, and Halfway serve the area. Private horse- and llama-packers lead trips into the deeper wilds of Eagle Cap Wilderness (the heart of the Wallowas) and Hells Canyon. For a top of the mountain perspective, the four-passenger gondola lift of Wallowa Lake Tram ascends 3,200 vertical feet to the summit of Mount Howard, at 8,256 feet. Byway spurs can extend the road trip to Imnaha, best known for its annual bear and snake feed, and to the Snake River at Copperfield. In these lonesome parts, self-reliance and a sense of humor are key.

Broad agricultural flats in the Grande Ronde Valley stretch to folded savannah ridges before giving way to more rolling terrain. Irrigation lines, railroad tracks, and farmhouses buried in cottonwood stands all contribute to views. Small towns tout their local high school teams, while the rustic screen doors of quaint general stores beg to be opened.

From Minam Hill, travelers descend into a dramatic canyon of basalt-terraced rims, heading for the Minam and Wallowa rivers. Past the Minam State Park turnoff, the satiny liquid band of the Wallowa River pairs with the byway. Where the valley broadens, travelers' pulses may be elevated by early views of the "Little Switzerland of North America"—the Wallowa Mountains.

Wallowa, Lostine, Enterprise, and Joseph serve as northern gateways to the Wallowas. The surrounding ranchland clears the way to grand mountain panoramas. Eagle Cap Wilderness encompasses 361,000 acres of these prized mountains, including more than fifty named peaks. The Matterhorn, the tallest, tops out at 9,845 feet. Crystalline rivers, high lakes, hanging valleys, ice fields, steeple-topped conifers, and alpine meadows seal the invitation.

The small town of Joseph has shaken off its dusty frontier image. Along the cobblestone walks of Main Street, more than a dozen life-like bronze sculptures glint under the mountain sun. Among the subjects are wild animals, Nez Perce Indians, cowboys, horses, and a barefoot girl on a garden walk. Nationally and internationally known foundries and galleries of all art forms rub shoulders with the shops of western sundries.

This 190-mile crescent off Interstate 84 sweeps east from La Grande (exit 261) on Oregon Highway 82 to Joseph, where it follows Highway 350, Forest Road 39, and Highway 86, returning to Interstate 84 at exit 302, just north of Baker City. Winter snow closes Forest Road 39.

In serpentine fashion, the Imnaha Wild and Scenic River works its way through the steep, arid steppes of Hells Canyon National Recreation Area.

The entire length of the Imnaha River is designated a wild and scenic river. This river journeys from the high Wallowa Mountains through forest and desert canyon before it empties into the Snake River.

A streetside collection of life-size bronze statues is the hallmark of Joseph, a town which successfully blends cowboy boots and art. The soaring eagle, the "Spirit of Joseph," greets travelers as they enter town.

Pack trains were used heavily in early forest management and travel; this group of packers paused at Sand Pass in Wallowa National Forest in 1911. (Courtesy of the United States Forest Service)

Joseph appears in John Villani's book, *100 Best Small Art Towns in America*.

At the head of the valley sits gorgeous Wallowa Lake, with its extensive state park and wilderness trails that follow the forks of the Wallowa River into the high country. The lake, cupped by high peaks and contained by a glacial moraine, shimmers a stunning blue and has a full line-up of recreational pursuits, with swimming, fishing, boating, and para-sailing. Chief Joseph's grave sits at the lake's foot.

The byway then leaves Joseph, following Highway 350 toward Imnaha, rounding the Wallowa Mountain centerpiece. Ranchland, beautiful barns, and mountain views precede the right turn onto Wallowa Mountain Road/Forest Road 39. (The untaken road straight ahead is the Imnaha spur.)

Wallowa Mountain Road twists out of the Little Sheep Creek drainage for an ear-popping ascent to Salt Spring Summit. In places, snag forests left by the Canal Fire of 1989 give the mountains a hoary stubble. Deer and elk can surprise travelers. The route passes from Wallowa-Whitman National Forest into Hells Canyon National Recreation Area. Past the Imnaha River recreation sites, where the route again climbs, a left turn on Forest Road 3965 travels 3 miles to Hells Canyon Overlook. Here, visitors find a paved walk, benches, interpretive panels, loads of wildflowers, and inspiring views on the canyon brink. An impressive 1.5 miles deep with an average width of 10 miles, Hells Canyon reigns as the deepest gorge in North America. Idaho's Seven Devils add a bold skyline to the humbling drop.

CHIEF JOSEPH AND THE NEZ PERCE

The Wallowa Valley was the traditional home of the usually peaceful Nez Perce (Nee-Mee-Poo) Indians. But the year 1877 changed all that, when trouble arising from the increase in white settlement led to a call for the U.S. military to evict the tribe from the valley. That order sent young Chief Joseph and the men, women, and children of his tribe on a desperate, 1,700-mile freedom quest to Canada. The path included a dangerous crossing of the unfettered Snake River in Hells Canyon during high water. Women, children, the sick, and the elderly rode atop horsehide rafts, pulled by riders on swimming horses. The tribe brought with them thousands of horses and cows. While great numbers of livestock drowned, no tribe member was lost. Chief Joseph nearly succeeded in gaining freedom for his people; he was captured just 40 miles from the Canadian border at Bear Paw, Montana. Although the descendants of the tribe are now dispersed, the Wallowas hold their cultural heart.

The town of Joseph, established in 1887, wears the name of young Chief Joseph, and two of the nearby peaks, Chief Joseph Mountain and Mount Howard, recall this page in history. The latter was named for the Army officer in charge of the eviction.

Each July since 1945, the town of Joseph has celebrated Chief Joseph Days, a tribute to the Nez Perce leader and the Old West. The tribal homecoming celebration, *TamKaLiks,* also in July, features a powwow and the Homecoming Dance in full regalia. September brings the Nez Perce art show. Small tribal museums in both Joseph and Wallowa preserve the Indian perspective.

The chief's father, old Chief Joseph, now rests at the foot of Wallowa Lake; his remains were relocated here in 1925, after his original grave had been raided. At the site, spiritual trinkets and mementos, such as feathers, beads, grass bundles, wood carvings, tobacco, bandannas, and dream catchers, honor the chief.

The Pine Creek drainage leads travelers out of the mountains and across the valley. Where Forest Road 39 meets Highway 86, a detour east leads to the Snake River at Copperfield, where camping is available. The byway heads west through Halfway and Richland, southern gateways to the Wallowa Mountains and the mountain line-up of recreation. Richland also provides access to Brownlee Reservoir on the Powder River. Views sweep across the rolling range and ranchland at the foot of the Wallowas and stretch west up the Powder River drainage to the Elkhorns.

At Flagstaff Hill, the National Historic Oregon Trail Interpretive Center has a fine museum, trails, the Meeker Monument, a wagon-encampment interpretive program, and views of original trail ruts. Summer walks on the sun-baked trails give visitors a tiny taste of the pioneer experience. As the byway hurries toward Interstate 84, it passes the obelisk commemorating the centennial of the Oregon Trail. From 1843 to 1869, some 250,000 pioneers braved the arduous trek.

At Interstate 84, Baker City sits 2 miles south; it's 41 miles north to close the loop at La Grande.

In the Elkhorn
Mountains,
Gunsight Mountain
watches over
Anthony Lake.
Trails originating
at or near the lake
travel to the more
remote mountain
areas.

GHOSTS OF GOLD
Elkhorn Scenic Byway

ROUTE 22

This 106-mile counterclockwise loop originates in the historic district of Baker City, traveling U.S. Highway 30 to Haines. It then follows Anthony Lakes Highway, Forest Road 73, Grant County Highway 24, and Oregon Highway 7. The loop cannot be completed in winter.

Against a forest and meadow backdrop, this loop revisits the mining heyday of the 1860s, beginning at Baker City, northeast Oregon's queen city of that era. Sumpter's small museums, narrow-gauge railroad, and dredge flesh-out the era, as do old cemeteries, a powerhouse, mill ruins, cabins, and tailings (the discarded rock from dredging). This drive also celebrates natural splendor at the Anthony Lake–Elkhorn Crest area and North Fork John Day Wild and Scenic River, both of which offer trails and wilderness access. On top of that, Elkhorn Scenic Byway is the springboard to two other byways: Blue Mountain (route 20) and Journey Through Time (route 19).

At the outbreak of the Civil War, gold, not war, fired-up folks in northeast Oregon. More than 10,000 mining claims were staked in Baker County, and Baker City became the heart of commerce. The surrounding forest and fertile farmland supplied the mines; railroads provided a link to markets. Baker City blossomed with elegant and respectable establishments, as well as "red-light district" saloons, bordellos, and gambling houses. Chinese immigrants, primarily single men who came to work the gold fields, swelled the population.

Today, 110 buildings compose the Baker City Historic District, with more than half fully restored to their Victorian elegance; a walking tour leads into the past. The Oregon Trail Regional Museum, a Chinese cemetery, and the 80.4-ounce Armstrong gold nugget displayed at the U.S. Bank Building help set the stage for byway travel. With a stop at the USFS office in town, travelers can gather information on the drive's hiking and camping recreation.

The byway traverses the ranchland at the eastern foot of the Elkhorn Mountains before taking the turn to enter these mountains at Haines. At Haines, the Eastern Oregon Museum and 1880s Pioneer Park contribute their own chapters to the unrolling history. Among the park's restored cabins is the county's first cabin, dating to 1861.

The route obtains close proximity to the jagged granite skyline of the Elkhorn Mountains. Below Gunsight Peak and The Lakes Lookout, Anthony Lake rivals wilderness lakes in beauty and backdrop. Camping is available at the lake and at its neighboring small lakes. Trails top peaks (8,000 footers), trace ridgelines, and visit backcountry lakes and meadows. Vistas and crisp mountain air invigorate hikers. Clark's nutcrackers feast on whitebark pine cones. The backcountry heights are wild enough for mountain goats, but more often it's the bellow of an elk that pierces the morning stillness. Since 1933, the powder at rustic Anthony Lakes Ski Area has attracted schussers and cross-country skiers.

The route twists across a 7,400-foot summit, traveling through forest and the silver legacy of the 1986 Clear Fire, which burned 6,000 acres. The route then descends to the North Fork John Day Wild and Scenic River, where it meets up with the Blue Mountain Scenic Byway.

As Forest Road 73 takes the Elkhorn tour south toward Granite, travelers can see part of a Chinese wall in about 7 miles. Chinese laborers leased the played-out placer claims, successfully reworking them by hand. The rock removed by the Chinese laborers was laid in walls parallel to streams. Dredge tailings, by contrast, line up perpendicularly. Elsewhere, an old mill ruin causes heads to turn.

Circling smoke from chimneys indicates the mining ghost town of Granite is no longer empty. A pioneer cemetery sits on the hill in town.

A visit to the 1908 Fremont Powerhouse, which fueled area mines, requires a 5-mile detour from town. Head right on Grant County Highway 24/Red Boy Road and, after 3.3 miles, bear right toward the powerhouse and Olive Lake.

Fremont Powerhouse is on the National Register of Historic Places. When staffing is available, it is open for tours. Since the roof's collapse in 1993, the plant has been fully restored with the help of grants, National Guard labor, and the tireless efforts of volunteers. The original marble console survived the collapse and the Guard has replicated its missing gauges. The associated housing, likewise, received a facelift and can be rented out from the USFS for overnight use.

Next is Sumpter, with its tale of the great fire of 1917, its historic town structures, and the Sumpter Valley Railroad and Dredge (state park units). Dynamite had to be used to stop the fire, but not before it had consumed 12 blocks of town. Shops now fill some of the surviving structures. The dredge sits where it was abandoned in the 1950s. It is one of the largest and most accessible gold dredges remaining in the United States today. It moved an average of 280,000 cubic yards of earth each month. Visitors can view it, inside and out; interpretive panels explain its workings and history. The Sumpter Valley narrow-gauge railroad provided the critical market link for the extracted ore and area logs. A restored section of track now carries summer train excursions—an unusual moving museum shrouded in a belch of steam.

From Sumpter, byway travelers parallel the train track south to Highway 7 (the Journey Through Time). Here, Elkhorn travelers pursue Highway 7 east along the Powder River back to Baker City. Philipps Lake, an irrigation reservoir, offers a last bid for overnight camping. Day-use sites along the river serve picnickers and river users.

ABOVE:

The Lower Crooked River National Back Country Byway hugs its namesake river as both snake through the basalt and juniper-sage habitat of the river canyon.

LEFT:

The aptly named Indian paintbrush adds a spark of red to the dusky palette of the Lower Crooked River canyon.

FACING PAGE:

In the narrow canyon of the Crooked Wild and Scenic River, the fractured Columbia River basalt creates fascinating skylines.

GOING CROOKED
Lower Crooked River National Back Country Byway

ROUTE 23

From U.S. Highway 26 in Prineville, this 45-mile byway heads south on Main Street/ Oregon Highway 27, heading up through the Crooked River Canyon and out through the desert, coming out at U.S. Highway 20, 36 miles east of Bend.

A crooked canyon road along a crooked river—what could be more arresting? The scenery is classic western frontier, but the narrow canyon of the Crooked River tips the concept of wide-open spaces on its ear. Above Bowman Dam and Prineville Reservoir, horizon-straining landscapes resume. On the brushy flats, the occasional antelope or jackrabbit can break the loneliness, but "jackalopes" remain elusive. The centerpiece of the tour, the seductive Chimney Rock Segment of the Crooked Wild and Scenic River lures sightseers, campers, and, most especially, fly-fishers.

Prineville, "Cowboy Capital of Oregon," is the drive's gatekeeper. This modest, western high-desert town has its roots in ranching, agriculture, and timber. The City of Prineville Railroad, which once hauled the ponderosa pines to mills, now rattles with the passing of a passenger excursion train. Other signature offerings are the pioneer history at Bowman Museum and events at Crook County Fairgrounds, including the annual Crooked River Roundup (a three-day rodeo event).

As the byway follows the east shore of the main stem of the Crooked River, rich irrigated pastures initially frame travel. Wranglers, ushering plaintive cows, sometimes share the byway. Upstream stretches the picturesque wild and scenic river segment. Both golden and bald eagles soar over this river, and ospreys and herons can satisfy their appetites for fish.

Despite modern changes, the Crooked River boasts an especially productive rainbow trout fishery. Steve Marx, a Bend-based biologist with the Oregon Department of Fish and Wildlife, puts the density of trout below Bowman Dam at 2,000 to 8,000 adult fish per river mile. Fly-lines dance onto the water, catching the glint of the sun—an image sure to inspire a rereading of *A River Runs through It* by Norman Maclean.

Formed by volcanoes some 1 million years ago, the canyon's picturesque basalt cliffs stretch 600 feet skyward. The corridor, barely 0.1 mile wide, forces a cozy pairing of river and road. Each bend recasts the visual image, with columnar buttes and crests, freestanding monoliths, mushroom-shaped overhangs, vertical ribs, and palisades. Mixed grasses, purple sage, and seasonal wildflowers spill across the juniper-studded terraces that stretch between the thick basalts. Within the canyon, shadow and light can play tricks on the eye, making features appear and disappear.

A series of camping and day-use recreation sites facilitate stopping. A single trail—the 1.5-mile Rim Trail—graces this narrow confine. It starts across from the Chimney Rock recreation site and climbs to the namesake monolith. This trail leads to the only elevated vantage of the river and gives a peek at the world beyond the canyon. Chimney Rock shoots 30 feet skyward from its saddle and 500 feet above the river.

The 1961 construction of Bowman Dam created Prineville Reservoir for the purpose of irrigation, but the impound also serves boaters and anglers, with both warm- and cold-water fisheries. Cupped by dusky juniper-sagebrush slopes, the lake covers up to 5 square miles, depending on water level. In winter, the reservoir area provides habitat for mule deer and bald eagles.

Beyond the reservoir, the byway twists and rolls, moving out of the river canyon and into the Bear Creek drainage. A few signed side roads branch from the route, but it is generally easy to follow. Spring wildflowers paint purple patches on the range.

Where the route crosses nearly dry Bear Creek, gravel replaces the pavement and much of the way to U.S. 20 is characterized by open road and dust in the review mirror. Solitary travel is common, but mule deer or a coyote can break the sameness of the sage desert.

A travelers' note: Rattlesnakes do dwell in the byway canyon terrain, so visitors should be alert when walking about. Also, because of the tinder conditions of the arid habitat, a ban on fires and smoking is in effect from June 1 through October 15.

THE ROAD LESS TRAVELED
Paulina/Izee Highway

A quiet alternative to U.S. 26 or U.S. 20, this backroad, not found in any tourist book, provides a relaxing traverse at the center of the state. The two-lane highway rolls across rural valley, pursuing the Crooked River and its headwaters between the Ochoco and Maury mountains. It then meets up with the South Fork John Day River before crossing into Malheur National Forest and following the Silvies River into Bear Valley. There are few potential stops: general stores, a pair of USFS campgrounds, and a USFS picnic area and nature trail where the route ends at U.S. 395. Windshield views offer thick pastures, isolated ranches, juniper-sagebrush hills,

ROUTE 24

This 118-mile paved backroad travels between U.S. Highway 26 in Prineville and U.S. 395 south of John Day. It is variously labeled Combs Flat Road, Paulina Highway, Paulina-Suplee Road, Paulina-Izee Road, or Crook County Highway 112/Grant County Highway 63.

Early logging was a labor-intensive operation for both loggers and their teams of stock. This is an 1890s logging operation in the Ochoco Mountains. (Courtesy of Crook County Historical Society)

ABOVE:

Isolated badland hills, painted in burgundy, black, and gold, rise up among the sage expanses of the Crooked River Valley. The most extensive badland beds lie in the John Day Country.

RIGHT:

Many backroads pass within easy reach of national forest lands. This odd arrangement of ponderosa pines sits in the Ochoco National Forest, off Paulina/Izee Highway.

LEFT:

Ranching is a mainstay of the Crooked River Valley, where weathered-board barns are common sights.

BELOW:

Wildlife sightings always add to the excitement of backroad travel, but unusual sightings, such as this owlet, make the trip especially fun.

painted badlands, rims, buttes, forested slopes, and the occasional mono-lith. It is a realm for deer and antelope and seekers of the road less trav-eled.

At the eastern outskirts of Prineville, travelers turn onto Combs Flat Road en route to Paulina, quickly passing a Prineville Reservoir turnoff. Valley ranchland precedes the ascent to the broad rolling terrace of Combs Flat, with its juniper woodlands. Where Eagle Rock overlooks the route, a closer look may reveal the rock's namesake, either perched or circling nearby. The route then pairs with the Crooked River, twisting through the canyon and tracing the valley.

Post, "the Center of Oregon," consists of the old grange and— what passes for a "mall" in these parts—a combination general store, tavern, post office, and gas pump. The sociable custodian may invite customers to answer the cowboy trivia question of the day. The enchantment of the establishment's old-fashioned country post office, agate-top bar, or mounted deer and elk heads may stretch out the purchase of an ice cream or postcard.

Isolated painted-badland features—all on private land or private pre-serve—poke through the desert slopes. The colored bands of red, gold, black, and tan resemble Navajo designs. These small beds are part of the John Day Formation, like the Painted Hills Unit of John Day Fossil Beds National Monument near Mitchell. Raptors, geese, killdeers, herons, and bald and golden eagles capture birders' attentions. The Crooked River provides an important wintering spot for bald eagles; March offers the best viewing.

Unincorporated Paulina—with a population too small for listing on state maps—is the biggest town on the backroad. Along with its multi-purpose general store, the town includes a church, a handful of residences, and a rodeo grounds. Besides the usual fare of ice cream and cold drinks, the mercantile sells local crafts and quilts. The town is a hub for rock-ounds. The surrounding mountains seclude Paulina limbcasts, Ochoco

Taken in Silvies Valley in 1923, this line up of buckaroos, include Peter French, a rancher who made his mark throughout Harney County. (Courtesy of Harney County Historical Society)

thundereggs, Maury Mountain jasper, and other sought-after rocks.

Paulina marks the last chance for services until U.S. 395. Towns farther east exist in name only.

A few miles east of Paulina, drivers come upon the junction with South Beaver Creek Road/Forest Road 58. Taking this route northeast and following signs will lead travelers to Sugar and Wolf Creek campgrounds, in 8.5 and 9 miles, respectively. The location of these campgrounds, about midway into the journey, is ideal for a picnic lunch. Both are restful retreats along babbling creeks. Ponderosa pines shade the camps, while meadow banks complement the spangling creeks.

Eastbound, the undulating Paulina/Izee Highway traverses broad valley basins, topping summits between drainages. Sage hills, rims, tables, and buttes make up the view. Beautiful willows and beaver-made pools accent creeks that run beside the road.

For a peek at the South Fork John Day River, travelers can turn north onto South Fork Road, a gravel national back-country byway that heads downstream along the river toward Dayville. The primary road trip proceeds east to Izee and U.S. 395. Pine-fir forests and a fire zone vary the views before giving way to the scenic beauty of Bear Valley, with its prairies frequented by deer and antelope. Across U.S. 395, Swick Creek Old Growth Interpretive Trail, less than a mile long and shaded by century-old ponderosa pine trees, offers a place to stretch the legs. The town of John Day sits north on U.S. 395.

During the 1910 harvest, threshing machines at Suplee are hard at work. (Courtesy of Crook County Historical Society)

PART V

THE SOUTHEAST:
OREGON OUTBACK

A lone hiker is dwarfed by the steep walls of Crack-in-the-Ground in the Four Craters Wilderness Study Area along Christmas Valley National Back Country Byway.

Ranch gates often provide a clue to the landowners' spirit or sense of humor. This gate top in Harney County is paired with a sunrise.

For all of its sagebrush expanses, the Oregon Outback rolls out a varied terrain, with large playa lakes, long-stretched rims, fault-block mountains, sand dunes, craters, lava flows, and stunning rock canyons. Pushing aside the sage are prairie and alpine meadows, aspen groves, juniper woodlands, ponderosa pine forests, and mixed forests at higher elevations. Wildlife is plentiful and, although the region has designated wildlife viewing spots, animals can be seen most anywhere. Coyote, antelope, deer, beaver, and elk can punch-up a tour, as can a host of migrant and resident birds, including great-horned owls, bald eagles, snow geese, sandhill cranes, orioles, and mountain bluebirds.

The land is remote and lightly populated; it is the place of the cowboy and the sagebrush philosopher. The people of the outback have a fierce spirit to match the fierce land. Cattle and sheep drives, branding, and foaling are some of the images of the outback frontier. Small towns engage backroad travelers with their simplicity and bygone hospitality.

But drives in the southeast call for special heed to vehicle preparation and packing. Help can be a long way off. Almost any road here fits the category of backroad. Fellow drivers are often few and far between. At times a "Twilight Zone" loneliness creeps over travelers, and the comfort of another pair of headlights will spark a reflexive wave.

ROAM ON THE RANGE
Oregon Outback Scenic Byway

ROUTE 25

This 156-mile ramble begins on Oregon Highway 31 south of La Pine (off U.S. Highway 97), turns south onto U.S. Highway 395 at Valley Falls Junction, and ends at the California-Oregon border.

Tighten the cinch, this is a drive into the western frontier, complete with ponderosa-pine forests, bunch grass, sagebrush, lowing cattle, alfalfa hay, cow ponies, and lonesome expanses. It is also a unique geological area with volcanic and fault features, vast alkaline lakes, long fault-block rims, hot springs, and even a geyser for good measure. Summer Lake Wildlife Area, which sits along the drive, is an important waterfowl migration site and a managed breeding site for trumpeter swans. Bordering the route, Fremont National Forest offers trails, camping, and lake and river recreation. At the towns of Silver Lake, Paisley, and Lakeview, ranger district offices serve travelers. Lakeview, at the southern end of the tour, is the journey's "metropolis."

Following the 1843 exploration route of John C. Fremont, lightly used Highway 31 is ideally suited for sightseeing. The wide cinder shoulders allow sightseers to pull aside for through travelers and marked turnoffs to geologic and forest features can suggest side trips on gravel roads. At Fort Rock Road, drivers have the option of taking an alternative fork through the town of Fort Rock, tracing part of the Christmas Valley National Back Country Byway (route 26).

Remaining on Highway 31, basalt rims, small cinder cones, and isolated buttes interrupt the expanses. This is a winter range for mule deer, but the browsers can be seen most anytime. Eagles, owls, antelopes, cranes,

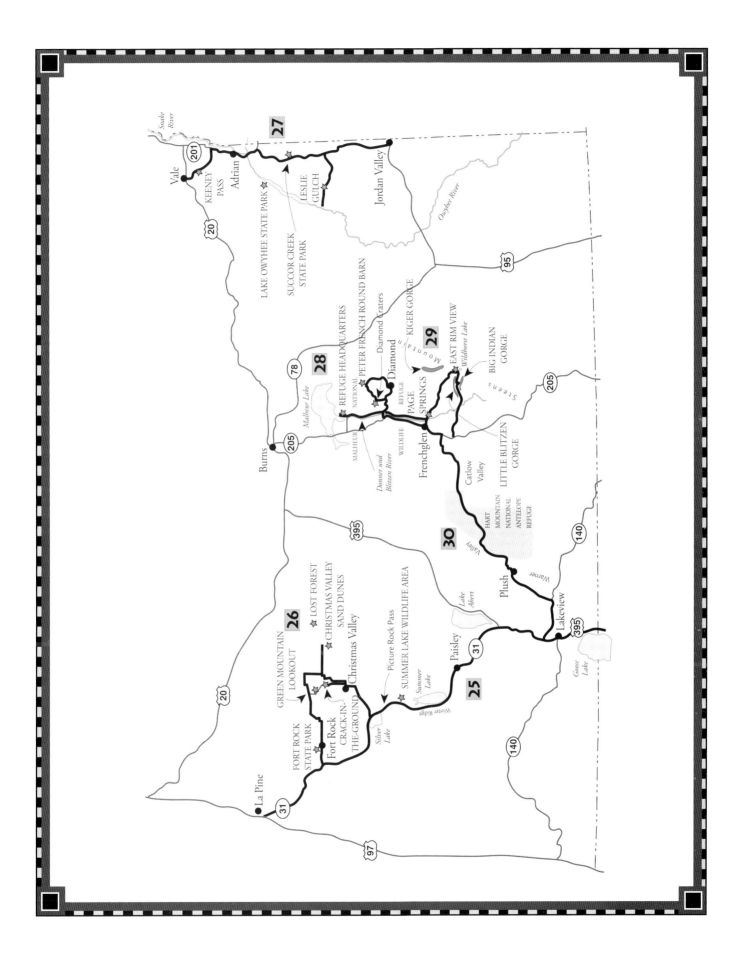

Snake River

201

Vale

20

KEENEY PASS

Adrian

LAKE OWYHEE STATE PARK

SUCCOR CREEK STATE PARK

LESLIE GULCH

27

Jordan Valley

Owyhee River

95

REFUGE HEADQUARTERS

PETER FRENCH ROUND BARN

Diamond Craters

KIGER GORGE

EAST RIM VIEW

78

28

MALHEUR NATIONAL WILDLIFE REFUGE

Malheur Lake

Diamond

PAGE SPRINGS

Wildhorse Lake

Steens Mountain

29

BIG INDIAN GORGE

205

Burns

205

Frenchglen

LITTLE BLITZEN GORGE

Donner and Blitzen River

Catlow Valley

205

395

HART MOUNTAIN NATIONAL ANTELOPE REFUGE

30

Warner Valley

140

Plush

Lakeview

395

LOST FOREST

CHRISTMAS VALLEY SAND DUNES

GREEN MOUNTAIN LOOKOUT

Christmas Valley

26

Picture Rock Pass

SUMMER LAKE WILDLIFE AREA

Lake Albert

Goose Lake

20

FORT ROCK STATE PARK

Fort Rock

CRACK-IN-THE-GROUND

Summer Lake

Winter Ridge

Paisley

25

31

Silver Lake

140

La Pine

31

97

Eastern Oregon byways have their own brand of traffic jams.

For the curious and the collector, backroads travel is ideal. The "Just Stuff" store in New Pine Creek at the California border is just one example of the many quirky and fun shops to explore.

Some of the signs that mark Oregon's backroads are works of art.

In Summer Lake Wildlife Area, Ana River Ranch offers a convenient place to stop and watch for wildlife. This barn can be seen for miles, rising above the marsh and sagebrush expanse.

The glassy surface of shallow Lake Abert reflects neighboring Abert Rim and the rocks that pierce the lake. The playa lake is actually a remnant of a vast ancient lake that covered much of the land along the Oregon Outback Scenic Byway.

coyotes, and elk have also been known to make appearances. Some wild-life interludes are humorous, such as when a rancher's calf decides to chase a 3-foot-tall sandhill crane, only to lose its gumption and legs as it meets up with the big, immovable bird. Designated wildlife viewing areas—Oatman Flat, Buck Creek, and Summer Lake—offer official places to stop.

Past the town of Silver Lake, drivers traverse broad, flat farmland, actually part of an ancient lakebed leftover from the time of glaciers. The open flat stretches to peaks and ridges, many of volcanic origin. As the route bends south, it skirts the mostly dry playa of Silver Lake, another remnant of that ancient lake. Atop Picture Rock Summit (milepost 63), elevation 4,830 feet, a footpath on the south side of the road leads to petroglyphs. Images on the trailside rocks depict both humans and animals. All such cultural resources are protected under law; visitors should take only pictures and avoid touching the images.

Expansive, alkaline Summer Lake sits at the base of Winter Ridge, both of which were named by the Fremont Expedition. At the southern end of the Summer Lake community sits the 18,000-acre Summer Lake State Wildlife Area, which offers primitive camping facilities. Autos travel on levees through the wildlife area, visiting marshes, salt flats, sagebrush areas, and open water channels; maps are stocked at the wildlife area's headquarters. Seasonally, side levees are open to walking. The site's School-house Lake Viewing Station and Ana River Ranch are likely stops. Sightings vary but can include trumpeter swans, snow geese, white pelicans, sandhill cranes, ducks, terns, pheasants, great-horned owls, avocets, and ibises. Mammal sightings can include deer, muskrats, coyotes, and foxes.

Ranching images, the blackened forest from the Winter Fire, and the distant glint of Summer Lake make up the views as the route proceeds south. Privately owned Summer Lake Hot Springs beckons with relaxing soaks. With the valley's marshes and broad shallow lakes comes an important food source for birds—the mosquito. In the spirit of "if you can't beat 'em, join 'em," travelers might wish to celebrate the needling insect at Paisley's Mosquito Festival held at the end of each July. Devised as a fundraiser for mosquito control, the festival boasts such signature events as the chicken-poop lotto and a draft-horse pull. The Chewaucan River west of town offers, camping, hiking, and fly-fishing for redband trout.

At Valley Falls Junction, the drive continues south via U.S. 395. A brief detour north on U.S. 395 traces the shoreline of Lake Abert, the large shallow lake at the foot of the Abert Rim. Hang gliders sometimes soar overhead; winds along the fault-scarp cliff are ideal for these gliders. Waterfowl, tiny by scale, dot the broad, open lake.

Established in 1888, Lakeview engages visitors with small-town appeal and a giant cowboy welcome. The north end of town holds Hunter Hot Springs and Old Perpetual Geyser, both privately owned. The geyser regularly belches steam 60 feet skyward and is visible from the drive. At Hunter Hot Springs Resort, visitors can pay to use the hot-springs pool, or they can take the road from the resort to a public parking lot for geyser viewing. A pair of local history museums offers retreat from the rain, sun, or wind. Their collections offer glimpses at pioneer and Indian artifacts, including sagebrush sandals dating back almost 10,000 years.

Funneling the route south out of town are a broad ranchland flat to the west and the 8,500-foot Warner Mountains to the east. Eventually, the glaring edge of Goose Lake adds to the western view. Seemingly too much for one state to handle, half of this 194-square-mile lake sits in California.

After viewing the lake for nearly 7 miles, travelers reach the community of New Pine Creek. Here they find the turnoff for Goose Lake State Park, which has camping and day-use facilities, and a boat ramp. The vast lake attracts its share of migratory waterfowl. Quail stroll through the campground, and mule deer seasonally feast on the park's abandoned orchard trees. To the south is California.

DESERT TIDINGS
Christmas Valley National Back Country Byway

This lonesome, sometimes dusty route encapsulates the story of a prehistoric inland sea, volcanic episodes, and hardy individuals. On the open sagebrush expanse, it visits unique geologic and natural features: Fort Rock, Crack-in-the-Ground, Christmas Valley Sand Dunes, and Lost Forest. Four wilderness study areas add to the neighborhood. In the town of Fort Rock, frontier buildings at the Homestead Village Museum reveal a bit about the dry-dirt farmers of the early 1900s. An old cemetery and abandoned homesteads further hint at life on the high-desert plain. Jackrabbits and wintering mule deer may hold the focus of visitors' binoculars; 30,000 mule deer winter in the area.

Fort Rock State Park sits north of the town of Fort Rock on County Road 5-11, but this volcanic feature has been a landmark from the journey's start. This imposing horseshoe fortress was formed some 100,000 years ago, when a large inland sea covered the area. After a pressure vent opened beneath the water, molten rock spewed forth, mingling with the cold lake water. The rock shattered and shot outward in a ring. As this tuff ring grew, it formed an island. Centuries of wave action then ate away at the island, leaving what is now Fort Rock. Its formidable wall rises 300 feet from the desert floor and shapes a ring 0.5-mile in diameter. The desert rises into the yawning gape of the arc. A trail enters the core of the fort, and raptors nest on the fort's ledges.

Back at Fort Rock, the route makes its way east and north from town. As the drive approaches and follows County 5-12B, travelers look out on two lava flows that are wilderness study areas: Devils Garden and Squaw Ridge. These areas sit within striking distance of the road, but there is little road edge on which to park safely. If a parking spot is found, hiking boots should be worn when exiting your vehicle; lava is brutal on any

ROUTE 26

This 93-mile byway tour begins on Fort Rock Road (Lake County Road 5-10) off Oregon Highway 31, about 32 miles southeast of La Pine. It then follows a sequence of Lake County roads: 5-11, 5-12, 5-12B, 5-14C, 5-14D, 5-14E, and BLM Road 6151, returning to 5-14C South. County Road 5-14 then carries the tour into Christmas Valley and County 5-14F returns drivers to Highway 31 southeast of Silver Lake. Parts are on gravel or dirt; routes are typically marked. The byway is accessible for high-clearance passenger vehicles, but having four-wheel-drive capability allows carefree travel. The route should be avoided when wet or snowy.

This rustic frontier church is part of the Homestead Village Museum in Fort Rock. The museum consists of a collection of historic buildings that recall the difficulties of life in the high desert.

LEFT:

The graveyards of the West evoke a simple beauty; this marker was found in Fort Rock Cemetery.

FACING PAGE, TOP:

Landmarks of civilization are far between in the open, arid expanse of Christmas Valley.

FACING PAGE, BOTTOM:

The shifting sands at Christmas Valley Sand Dunes shape an ever-changing canvas.

other type of sole. Devils Garden is the largest and most extensive of the flows. Its surface consists of pahoehoe, a smooth, ropey lava resulting from a slow cooling. A juniper woodland precedes the crusty aa lava of the Squaw Ridge Lava Flow. A rapid cooling created this chunky form of lava.

Along the Squaw Ridge flow, drivers encounter a junction. The rough 17-mile BLM route to the south is for high-clearance vehicles only. It travels past Green Mountain Lookout, Four Craters Lava Flow, and Crack-in-the-Ground, with the route growing especially rough along the flow. Drivers will have a second chance to access Crack-in-the-Ground later in the tour.

Despite the "alternate" label, the primary route for passenger vehicles proceeds forward before turning south on County 5-14C. Tumbleweeds dot the fences, and the frontier outback stretches as far as the eye can see. An old homestead with a tattered cloth blowing in a vacant doorway reminds drivers of bygone days.

At the junction with County 5-14D, drivers can strike east 11.5 miles across the sagebrush desert, following County Roads 5-14D and 5-14E and BLM Road 6151 to the rail-fenced parking area and stopping point for Christmas Valley Sand Dunes and Lost Forest. The final leg on BLM Road 6151 is on dirt and can be impassable when wet. This route should be avoided altogether with low-clearance vehicles. From the parking area, only those with four-wheel drive can continue on posted roads.

Cross-country foot travel leads into the dunes to the south or relict ponderosa-pine forest to the east and north. Hikers should carry a good supply of water and possess a good sense of direction. The best way to avoid becoming lost is to make frequent note of landmarks and never stray farther than can be safely backtracked. Jeep roads offer established routes. Because off-road vehicles share the dunes, hikers need to be alert when topping ridges, rounding slopes, or approaching potential blind spots.

Despite the tire tracks rolling over the bare contours, the 15,000 acres of dunes are a wilderness study area. Ash and pumice from the eruption of Mount Mazama compose the dunes, which can top 60 feet. In the adjoining Lost Forest Research Natural Area, off-road travel is prohibited. Comprising nearly 9,000 acres, this area houses a unique vestige of ponderosa pines. The climate here was once moist, and these trees were abundant; strangely, though, the Lost Forest pines survive despite inadequate rain and moving sand. Although the homestead boom of the early 1900s depleted the isolated stand, the period was short-lived and cutting was halted. Among the Lost Forest pines grow some of the largest junipers in Oregon.

Back on County 5-14C, the byway continues toward Christmas Valley. Soon after turning west on County 5-14 comes the junction with BLM Road 6109D. Travelers in vehicles with good clearance can follow this spur about 7 miles to the trailhead parking for Crack-in-the-Ground; a short trail leads to this geologic feature. The result of a tension fracture, Crack-in-the-Ground appeared nearly 1,000 years ago and has little changed. The slot stretches 2 miles, reaches a depth of 70 feet, and in a couple of places is barely more than shoulder-width across. Cool recesses can hold ice—a prized commodity harvested by desert homesteaders. Footpaths lead along and through the slot; each perspective elicits a "wow." Mountain bluebirds flit between area junipers.

Christmas Valley, a small ranching community of about 500 families, helps dispel the isolation of the road and offers basic services. The town's claim to fame is its postmark; people from other parts of the state bring their holiday cards to the town's post office for mailing. From town, drivers head south toward Black Hills and then southwest to Highway 31.

PIONEERS AND PALISADES
Leslie Gulch–Succor Creek Backroad

The Oregon Trail, superlative canyons, the Owyhee River and Reservoir, and the Basque country of Jordan Valley entice travelers to this remote edge of Oregon at the Idaho border. Bridging the attractions are irrigated farmlands of wheat, potatoes, sugar beets, and onions; range lands of cattle; and sage-grass hills and flats. The canyons of Succor Creek and Leslie Gulch captivate with their dramatic high-rise cliffs, spires, and subtle shades of color. Rock arches, honeycombs, windows, and shields vary impressions, while the bighorn sheep in Leslie Gulch can put a flourish on the canyon signature. The Malheur, Owyhee, and Snake rivers flood life into this otherwise parched region.

Vale (population 2,000) is the biggest service community on the drive and holds the BLM office, where drivers can inquire about roads, maps, and sites. The walls of local businesses are adorned with murals, recapturing moments on the Oregon Trail. The Rinehart Stone House, on the National Register of Historic Places, was the area's first permanent building. It served as a stagecoach inn and a safe harbor during the 1878 Bannock Paiute uprising.

Lytle Boulevard alternately traces or parallels the Oregon Trail. Concrete obelisks or BLM stakes mark the historic route. Time and erosion have worn the wagon tracks into deep ruts, softened by grass. Humanizing the saga are side stops, starting with Henderson Grave, reached by a marked side road in less than a mile. Beyond the gate, the original etched stone and a contemporary marker rest among the boulders. One version has it that Henderson tragically died of thirst, never knowing he was within striking distance of the Malheur River. Another has it he died of black measles, and a blacksmith etched the death notice on the rock. Whatever the version, such stories were common on the Oregon Trail. It's been said that for every mile there's a grave.

This 115-mile backroad travels between Vale on U.S. Highway 20/ 26 and Jordan Valley on U.S. Highway 95. From Vale, go south on Glenn Street, which becomes Lytle Boulevard, turn east on Enterprise Avenue, and follow Oregon Highway 201 south to the marked turn for Succor Creek Road. The route adds a spur on Leslie Gulch Road about 10 miles after Succor Creek State Park Campground, and then resumes south on Succor Creek Road to U.S. 95, which it follows south to Jordan Valley. Canyon routes are improved gravel; high-clearance vehicles are recommended. Avoid this route when the weather is wet or snowy.

ABOVE:

Leslie Gulch along the Owyhee River rests well off the beaten path, but rewards travelers with isolation, a fanciful realm of multihued volcanic-tuff cliffs, and chance sightings of bighorn sheep.

RIGHT:

Jordan Valley is cowboy country, where a good horse and a sound rope are key.

The buildings of Vale are decorated with murals depicting the history of the Oregon Trail. The mural collection numbers twenty-five and continues to grow. The Trappers *by Norm Comp depicts a camp along the Malheur River.*

The people of eastern Oregon often feel left out of state government, and this retired outhouse in Adrian provides a medium for a little political humor.

Keeney Pass serves as the primary interpretive station along this stretch of the Oregon Trail. Here, panels with journal entries bring the migration to life. A short trail tops the site's hill; the view stretches from the Snake River to Vale—a distance that would have been a full day's journey for the pioneers. August travelers can experience the heat the pioneers faced, but will have to imagine the choking dust, the fatigue from 1,600 spirit-breaking miles, and the weighty prospect of 300 to 400 miles still to come.

Drivers will encounter several opportunities to add a side trip to Owyhee Reservoir and its state park. They sit southwest off the backroad; marked side roads point the way through the agricultural lands. The reservoir is the longest in Oregon, stretched across 53 miles. Red-orange cliffs contain the impound, at times squeezing the pool to only a mile in width. The park campground is popular with boaters and offers deciduous trees for shade.

The small crossroads community of Owyhee serves up the last chance for gas; Adrian is the last chance for food, water, and other necessities.

With a cloud of dust, Succor Creek Road takes the tour into the hinterlands, crossing arid flats punctuated by picturesque desert hills. Despite its remoteness, the route receives regular traffic from rockhounds, ranchers, and sightseers. The green ribbon of tree-lined Succor Creek offers an eye-catching contrast to the dry grass and sage. Where travelers enter the canyon of the state-park lands, cliffs of red, orange, buff, and desert-varnish black contain the backroad and waterway. The chiseled skyline reveals natural skylights, hammers, rugged teeth, and chunky forms. Each bend in the road spells expectation. The rustic state-park campground is an oasis.

The turnoff onto Leslie Gulch Road (a right turn) leads into another canyon wonderland of drama and surprise. The Leslie Gulch Area's volcanic ash shapes a phantasmagoric realm, where rocks conjure images ranging from artichokes to heavy plated dinosaurs. When rubberneck viewing from the vehicle grows tiring, travelers can hike up the side-canyon washes (natural travel aisles). Slocum Gulch (behind the primitive campground at the road's end) and Juniper Gulch (on the way in) are popular avenues to explore. Bighorn sheep can be spied in each. Golden eagles, coyotes, chukar, and mule deer are other canyon dwellers. On rambles, foot travelers must be alert for ticks and rattlesnakes.

The Leslie Gulch Area is an 11,653-acre BLM Area of Critical Environmental Concern. Special regulations protect the scenery and habitat. The volcanic tuff of the canyon is a product of two eruptions, Mahogany Mountain and Three Fingers, from more than 15 million years ago. Leslie Gulch Road comes to a halt at Owyhee Reservoir, the appearance of which varies greatly depending on the season and rain year. Backtracking is required to continue the journey south. The area's rare endemic plants excite botanists.

Jordan Valley wraps up the road trip. Its history began with a gold discovery in 1863; the town later served as a stage link between California and Idaho. The arrival of Texas longhorns in the late 1860s launched the area's cattle industry. The Basques, whose traditional home was in Europe's West Pyrenees, arrived in the 1890s and established a thriving colony. They were skilled sheep raisers, masons, miners, and merchants. The masons' handiwork is revealed in the town's stone Pelota Fronton, a ball court for a sport that resembles American handball. The court was originally built in 1915 and was a Basque gathering place; today it's on the National Register of Historic Places.

COWBOYS, CRANES, AND CRATERS
Malheur National Wildlife Refuge–Diamond Loop

Vast shallow lakes; a seasonal chaos of waterfowl; craters; and a rich ranching legacy help shape the tale of this backroad duo. The underpinnings of the American West—solitude, wide open spaces, the creak of a turning windmill, wailing coyotes—are strong here in the high desert. For those traveling by four-wheel-drive vehicle, there is the chance sighting of wild horses racing across the plain in a cloud of dust. Historic inns and the far-flung structures of the historic Peter French Ranch (P Ranch) capture a bit of the romance of this hard-bitten land.

Considered one of the ten best birding spots in the nation, Malheur National Wildlife Refuge covers a whopping 187,000 acres and hosts more than 320 bird species and nearly 60 mammals. The first records of the bountiful birdlife appear in military journals from the 1850s. Many birders find the headquarters—with its feeders, trees, and pond—a destination in itself, especially in warbler season. Bird sightings in the refuge vary with the season and the time of day; common sightings include grebes, herons, pheasants, hawks, owls, swans, snow geese, and ducks.

The distinctive chortle of sandhill cranes can draw eyes skyward. The large birds return in mid February for an April nesting, and they depart in October. During fall staging, they often gather in the grain fields off Diamond Lane. The refuge supports 10 percent of the adult population of the once numerous Central Valley greater sandhill cranes, with 250 breeding pairs. The Central Valley population, the westernmost population, ranges from California through British Columbia to Alaska.

The drive's Center Patrol Road draws a bisecting line south through the refuge, briefly veering out onto Highway 205. Views take in Coyote Buttes, Diamond Craters, and Steens Mountain. Travelers journey through marsh and brush habitats, visiting the channeled Donner und Blitzen River and some roadside ponds. Side roads lead to Petroglyph Rock and Krumbo Reservoir or to the lofty perspective of Buena Vista Overlook. The mix of wild and cropped areas indicates wildlife management strategies.

An old observation tower, a favorite with roosting vultures, and the Peter French Long Barn wrap up the Center Patrol Road part of the tour. The barn, on the National Register of Historic Places, is one of several structures recalling P Ranch, which was run by the Peter French–Hugh

This 51-mile drive starts east off Oregon Highway 205, at Malheur National Wildlife Refuge Headquarters (32 miles southeast of Burns). It follows the refuge's Center Patrol Road (with a brief stretch on Highway 205) south to Steens Mountain Loop Road, where it turns west to Highway 205. On Highway 205, the route heads north to Diamond Lane, which takes the tour east across the Malheur refuge to the Diamond Loop junction; travel is clockwise, north on Lava Bed Road. At the junction near Peter French Round Barn, a right turn on Happy Valley Road begins the loop's return through Happy Valley and Diamond, passing an optional spur into the Kiger Mustang Management Area for people with four-wheel-drive vehicles. Parts of the drive are on dirt or gravel.

Many backroads, particularly in the Oregon Outback, roll out long empty stretches. Here, Diamond Loop National Back Country Byway travels across lightly populated Harney County, which has less than one person per square mile.

Malheur National Wildlife Refuge, south of Burns, is a major birdwatching spot. From fall through spring, migrant and wintering populations of waterfowl swell the bird count. The snow geese are crowd pleasers.

Peter French built a ranching empire in Harney County. One of his more innovative ideas was the construction of a round barn, where horses could be trained and exercised during the harsh eastern Oregon winters. Shown here are the juniper, umbrella-like supports of the round barn.

Glenn cattle empire of the late 1800s and stretched across 200,000 acres. P Ranch had a colorful saga that included vaqueros, land squabbles, and a shooting.

Where Center Patrol Road meets Steens Mountain Loop Road, a left turn leads to Page Springs, a popular BLM campground. The selected route heads right (west) to Frenchglen and Highway 205. Enfolded by picturesque old shade trees, the tiny crossroads community of Frenchglen sprang up in response to the area ranches' need for services. The charming American-foursquare structure with the screened porch is the historic Frenchglen Hotel. It has served travelers to the Steens Mountain–Malheur Basin area since the 1920s. Now part of the state park system, the hotel continues to rent rooms and serve family-style meals.

By following Highway 205 north 20 miles, visitors reach the Diamond Loop kiosk and the byway turnoff onto Diamond Lane, which cuts east back across the Malheur National Wildlife Refuge to the loop junction; travel is clockwise.

First up is the 5-mile auto tour into 17,000-acre Diamond Craters Outstanding Natural Area. This otherworldly area reveals a diversity of volcanic forms. Its beginnings trace back 25,000 years to when cracks formed in the earth's crust and lava oozed forth, creating a pool 6 miles in diameter. Later volcanic episodes then swelled and burst the hardened mantle, with the more violent episodes creating spatter cones, cinder cones, and craters. Lava tubes and a water-filled maar (a broad crater formed by shallow explosions) are other discoveries. Chunky and ropey lava, along with cinders, vary footing; boots serve foot travelers well here. Lichens and dottings of grass, shrubs, and wildflowers add to this devil's playground.

The route north gathers more impressions of the flow before retiring into the sagebrush expanses and desert rims. The area is wild enough for coyotes and antelope. At the loop junction with gravel Happy Valley Road, a quick jog north and east leads to the Peter French Round Barn.

Built of native rock and juniper in the early 1880s, this barn was used during the bitter Eastern Oregon winters to exercise and break saddle horses for the Peter French Ranch. The round shape was ideal for the purpose, allowing fluid movement. Like a walled giant umbrella, the barn measures 100 feet in diameter. Twelve giant junipers, secured from the Blue Mountains 150 miles away, support its roof; the central pole is 35 feet tall. The barn is listed on the National Record of Historic Places.

The loop resumes, rounding first into Happy Valley and then over the plateau into Diamond Valley. Scenes include pastures, sagebrush, big cottonwoods, and willow drainages. Spring foals and calves and a host of birds on the flooded bottomlands animate the private ranches.

Between the two valleys is the marked turnoff for the 11-mile spur into the Kiger Mustang Management Area. Reserved for four-wheel-drive vehicles, this rough, dry-weather road ends at an overlook of beautiful lower Kiger Creek Gorge, where wild horses can be spied. West out of Burns, alternative viewing can be found at the BLM wild horse corrals, where animals from the surplus herd can be adopted.

As the loop draws to its close, visitors enter Diamond (population three), a place rooted in time and mostly forgotten, save for the historic Hotel Diamond, which still caters to the public. In this isolated reach, the town was once a central gathering place for ranchers and sheepherders. Here, they could secure supplies, find a soft bed, and wash the dust from their throats.

From town, drivers can return to the refuge or to Highway 205 and Burns.

KIGER WILD HORSES

Horses on the North American continent had become extinct in 8,000 B.C., but were reintroduced with the arrival of the Spaniards. The Kiger wild horses, direct descendants of these sixteenth-century Spanish mustangs, have a characteristic stocky build, a tailbone stripe, zebra-like bar marking on hocks, and dark manes. These traits are more pronounced in some descendants than others. Colors range from chocolate brown to buckskin to gray. The horses were and are prized for their endurance, intelligence, and agility—qualities that serve them well in this trying land.

An important symbol of the American frontier, the free-roaming herd is protected. But to keep the herd from overwhelming its range, surplus horses are culled and adopted out to private individuals. The Bureau of Land Management wild horse corrals, outside of Burns, provide interim housing. Here, the horses are medically examined, treated, and cataloged before being put up for adoption. During adoption periods, days are set aside for potential adopters to get a closer view of the horses. Tours also can be arranged.

OVERLEAF:
This southern view from Steens Mountain National Back Country Byway sweeps across the wide open juniper-dotted sage expanse of the Basin and Range. The Basin and Range geographic area is characterized by long mountains separated by dry, flat expanses.

At Frenchglen (60 miles south of Burns on Oregon Highway 205), the byway heads east on Steens Mountain Loop Road (improved gravel), climbing 28 miles to the mountain's summit. People in high-clearance and four-wheel-drive vehicles can then continue down the south side of Steens (part of which is rough) to Highway 205, where the route returns north 10 miles to Frenchglen, a 66-mile loop. People in conventional passenger vehicles must backtrack down from the summit to Frenchglen. From there, they can reach the south side of the mountain, heading 10 miles south on Highway 205 to the southern terminus of Steens Mountain Loop Road and continuing east up the mountain as far as South Steens Campground (another 19 miles). The byway route usually opens in July and closes in October.

On this backroad, travelers shoot for the sky on the highest climbing road in Oregon. The route travels from the 4,100-foot elevation of the high-desert floor to the 9,700-foot elevation at the summit of Steens Mountain. The ascent counts off vegetation zones: sagebrush, juniper, aspen, upland prairies, and tortured subalpine. Panoramic viewing and brink-of-the-rim overlooks of the mountain's deep glacial gorges captivate onlookers. The nearly vertical craggy scarp face is home to bighorn sheep; Kiger Gorge secludes descendants of the sixteenth-century Spanish mustangs. Antelope, mule deer, elk, sage grouse, and mountain bluebirds are among the more commonly spied creatures. Much of Steens is designated wilderness; a few inholdings remain private, but throughout, the spirit is wild.

Frenchglen launches the journey and offers a last call for gas and services. From the town, the route heads east on Steens Mountain Loop Road, skirting the southern edge of Malheur National Wildlife Refuge (see route 28, "Cowboys, Cranes, and Craters").

Along the Donner und Blitzen River, Page Springs Campground offers a pleasing overnight base at the foot of the mountain. The glistening desert stream carries native redband trout, enticing fly-fishers. The long-distance, cross-country Desert Trail flows through camp. One for the expert, this unusual trail-less trail travels cairn to cairn and has associated maps and brochures that take hikers from compass point to compass point. Farther up slope, Fish Lake and Jackman Park Campgrounds offer alternative base camps. Fulfilling similar needs on the south side of the mountain are the adjacent South Steens family and equestrian campgrounds.

Steens Mountain, the largest fault-block mountain in North America, stretches 30 miles long and shoots up a vertical mile from the Alvord Desert. The byway ascends the broad, gradual plateaus of the western flank, passing through the distinctly drawn vegetation zones. Foot travel is primarily cross-country; old jeep trails and rims suggest logical routes. Early views stretch both north across the high desert and east to the High Steens, the dramatic upper mountain. Spring, summer, and fall tumble over each other in a somersault of color and splendor.

The mountain's history encompasses the Native American and Basque cultures and early day ranching. Big Indian Gorge was the site of a summer Indian encampment. The Native Americans here would camp, hunt, fish, gamble, and race horses. By contrast, the Basque sheepherders led a solitary existence. Site names and the shepherds' notices and bawdy drawings carved into aspens recall the Basque presence, but the carvings are falling victim to time. Steens' cattle history also is being rewritten. Steens Mountain Wilderness is the first wilderness area in the nation to be completely closed to cattle raising.

The signatures of this mountain are the incomparable U-shaped glacial gorges and the plunging east wall. Kiger Gorge Viewpoint offers the first overlook. Although wild horses can sometimes be seen in the canyon bottom, the true majesty is the rugged mountain gash, its rounded bottom, the rim's Gun Sight notch, and the overall scale. The passing of an antelope or a golden eagle accentuates the wildness.

As the byway passes between the big escarpment of the eastern face and the headwalls of the glacial gorges, breath-stealing views compound. Little Blitzen Gorge strikes awe with its dramatic terraced-rock headwalls and its steep green bowl parted by the sparkle of an ice-melt stream. The gorge frames a western view to the high desert, one of the most magnificent panoramas in the state.

Side roads lead to the East Rim and the summit, both of which offer dizzying looks at the mountain's vertical east flank plunging to the alkaline basin of the Alvord Desert. Clear-day views stretch from East Rim to the Owyhee Uplands. Unexpected sightings can include ledge-hopping bighorn sheep, deer cooling off in a snowfield, or a peregrine falcon on the hunt. At the summit parking area, a foot trail leads to Wildhorse Lake, a small, stunning cobalt pool that serves wildlife and provides a looking glass to the rugged neighborhood.

Big Indian Gorge keeps the wonder going with its own gee-whiz factor, as the loop road traces the divide between Little Blitzen and Big Indian Gorge. Where the road narrows and grows rougher, 5 miles past the summit junction, conventional vehicles must turn around. The southern descent from the mountain is fairly steep and very rough in spots, but views are grand and a couple of turnouts allow for slower appreciation. Mountain mahogany takes the place of aspen, which favor the north face.

RIDDLE BROTHERS RANCH NATIONAL HISTORIC DISTRICT

The Bureau of Land Management oversees and protects the natural and cultural resources of the 1,120-acre Riddle Brothers Ranch National Historic District. This ranch recounts the homestead legacy of Steens Mountain. Here, in the 1900s, three bachelor brothers dwelled and worked, raising cattle and horses in the Little Blitzen Valley. Each brother kept a house in the canyon; many of the original ranch structures remain. An attractive rock rim overlooks the main two-story ranch house and barn.

The road into the ranch is found 0.1 mile west of South Steens Horse Camp; drivers can travel 1 mile to the gate. From there, it is another 1.25 miles on foot to the ranch. Presently, buildings are open during the daytime hours; a caretaker is on site. Looking at the tools (many handmade; some fashioned from juniper and old metal), the "luxuries" (an old refrigerator and upholstered rocking chair), and the necessities (rat poison and mousetraps), visitors come to the conclusion that although the ranchers' lives were spartan, the men were innovative. It's amazing what they could do with just a piece of wire. The collection spans fifty years.

The attractive Donner und Blitzen Wild and Scenic River, flows at the base of Steens Mountain. Such waterways are the lifeblood of the desert plain, attracting wildlife. Cairn-to-cairn travel on the Desert Trail takes seasoned hikers along this waterway.

This relic from the working ranch hangs on the wall of the Frederick Riddle House in the Riddle Ranch National Historic District at Steens Mountain. In the early 1900s, the bachelor Riddle brothers operated a horse and cattle ranch in the isolated Little Blitzen Valley.

Steens Mountain is the highest drive-to point in Oregon and the views are stunning. This Steens Mountain panorama overlooks Wildhorse Lake, a critical watersource for wildlife, and spans east across the Alvord Desert. The upper elevation of Steens Mountain is home to bighorn sheep.

Trails on the south side of the mountain invite visitors into Little Blitzen Gorge, Big Indian Gorge, or Riddle Brothers Ranch National Historic District, all in the vicinity of South Steens Campground. The BLM stakes that indicate wilderness areas also suggest possible sites for cross-country hiking.

The drive then leaves the mountain, following the high-desert plain down to Highway 205. From there, the loop closes 10 miles north in Frenchglen.

WHERE THE ANTELOPE PLAY
Lakeview to Steens Mountain National Back Country Byway

ROUTE 30

This 111-mile paved and gravel backroad travels between U.S. Highway 395 in Lakeview and Oregon Highway 205 in Frenchglen, crossing over Hart Mountain. It follows Highway 140 East, Plush Cut-off Road (Lake County 3-13), Hart Mountain Road (Lake County 3-12), and Highway 205. In winter, call the Hart Mountain National Antelope Refuge about road conditions over Hart Mountain. (The phone number is listed in the "Suggested Resources" at the back of the book.)

This backroad shakes free of the trappings of civilization. Once out of Lakeview, the only touchstone is the tiny crossroads town of Plush. The route traverses Warner Canyon, Camas Prairie, the Warner Lakes Basin, and Hart Mountain National Antelope Refuge. It then surrenders to even less visited reaches before meeting up with Oregon Highway 205 and continuing north to Frenchglen, at the western base of Steens Mountain.

Ranchland and juniper-sage hills shape the avenue into Warner Canyon, where ponderosa pines and the willow-lined creek add to the views. Between Warner Canyon and Camas Prairie rises Warner Pass, where travelers find sno-parks, a ski area, and access routes into Fremont National Forest. The national forest can divert travelers with its hiking and camping opportunities. Its aspen groves are a popular draw in autumn. At Camas Prairie, the spring bloom of the namesake flower is a purple welcome mat that grabs attention. The camas is a member of the lily family; the sweet edible bulb of the blue-purple flower was a vital foodstuff for Native Americans.

By contrast, the dusky palette of the low-sagebrush prairie carries the cut-off road toward the distant 3,000-foot-high escarpment of Hart Mountain. Like Steens Mountain, Hart Mountain is a fault-block mountain. After a long spell of sagebrush, a rimrock aisle leads into Plush. The tiny town has only a general store/saloon, a gas pump, and a small park with water and privies, but enjoys a budding reputation among rockhounds for its local "diamond"—sunstone, a tiny crystal that glistens under the high-desert sun. For diamond seekers, the BLM maintains a public collection site outside of Plush. Maps are available at the Lakeview District office; access requires a high-clearance vehicle.

At the foot of Hart Mountain, the route arcs into the 51,000-acre Warner Lakes Basin, one of the most significant closed-lake basins in the western United States. It stretches 40 miles north, spans 5 miles wide, and enfolds shallow lakes, marsh, and uplands critical to migrating and breeding waterfowl. The basin holds one of the four remaining nesting colonies for white pelicans in the Pacific states. The appearance of this great basin wetland varies greatly with water level. Dry spells enhance its overall health, keeping it oxygenated and productive.

Hart Lake offers the initial greeting. Desert plateaus, rims, and mountains complement views. Canada geese, dabblers, coots, red-wing and yellow-headed blackbirds, and wrens animate the various habitats, while coyotes sound from the canyons of Hart Mountain. Interpretive panels at roadside turnouts introduce habitat and history.

At the mountain's foot, basalt boulders hide petroglyphs. Obsidian flakes can be detected on the Hart Mountain rim. Warner Lakes Basin, with its ample fish and wildlife, was well used by Native Americans. Tule rafts and decoys have dated an Indian presence back as far as 9,000 years.

Side canyons of Hart Mountain offer rugged cross-country hikes; jeep trails offer alternative avenues to walk. A waterfall can be found in Degarmo Canyon, but accessing the canyon mouth requires a high-clearance vehicle. Bighorn sheep roam the upper escarpment reaches, but sightings require binoculars and luck.

The route changes to gravel for the ascent. Atop Hart Mountain, travelers find the Hart Mountain National Antelope Refuge Headquarters and Hot Springs Campground, the only developed spots in the Hart Mountain National Antelope Refuge.

The pronghorn antelope population once numbered 30 to 40 million, but the species did not fare well with civilization. Railroad tracks caused many to starve, because the antelopes refused to cross the tracks that stood between their winter and summer ranges. Others fell victim to poisonous baits put out for wolves and coyotes. Range pressures further depleted antelope numbers. In seventy-five years' time, the once widespread range of the pronghorn antelope was reduced to only a handful of strongholds. Hart Mountain was one.

Together with Sheldon National Wildlife Refuge, 30 miles southeast in Nevada, and the lightly settled Catlow Valley in Oregon, Hart Mountain shapes a critical unbroken winter and summer range for the pronghorn. At Hart Mountain, the antelope linger spring through fall, giving birth in May and June. As the byway traverses Hart Mountain's broad sagebrush top, the attractive animals can be spied alone or in groups. Because of the antelopes' keen vision, they are often on the move before being spotted and they travel at a quick pace.

A lonesome expanse follows as the road leaves the mountain. Sagebrush stretches as far as the eye can see. In Catlow Valley, the few buildings only emphasize the emptiness of the expanse. Distant views include Catlow Rim, the picturesque Pueblo Mountains to the south, and Steens Mountain to the north.

At Highway 205, the byway heads north for Steens and Frenchglen, traveling parallel to Pickett Rim.

Hart Mountain, home to Hart Mountain National Antelope Refuge, is a fault block mountain with an imposing front cliff. The pronghorn antelope range the top and broad backside of this mountain. Hart Mountain, Catlow Valley, and Nevada's Sheldon National Wildlife Refuge shape an unbroken range for the antelope.

East of the Cascades, aspens and cottonwoods put on a golden show in autumn. This aspen graces Stairstep Spring in Fremont National Forest.

Rustic corrals, such as this one at Post Meadow in Hart Mountain National Antelope Refuge, recall the ranching legacy in eastern Oregon.

INDEX

Abert Rim, *131, 132*

Agness, *76, 77, 80*

Alder Flat Trail, *52*

Alsea Falls, *32, 34*

Anthony Lake, *115, 116*

Applegate Trail, *33, 68*

Astoria, *12, 14–17*

B&B Complex Fire, *60*

Baker City, *92, 100, 109, 113, 116, 117*

Bandon, *68, 76, 80*

Banks-Vernonia Linear State Trail, *15, 16*

Barlow Road, *45*

Bayocean Peninsula, *20*

Benton County Historical Museum, *33*

Benton County Scenic Loop, *32–33, 34*

Big Indian Gorge, *148, 149, 152*

Big Tree, *80*

Blue Mountains, *92, 101, 104, 105*

Blue Mountain Scenic Byway, *105–108, 116, 117*

Breitenbush River, *49, 53*

Bridge Creek Wildlife Area, *105, 108*

Bridges, *31, 35, 36–37, 39, 53*

Cape Kiwanda, *20*

Cape Lookout, *20*

Cape Meares, *19*

Cape Perpetua, *29*

Captain Jack, *68, 85*

Cascade Lakes Scenic Byway, *64–65*

Cascade Mountains, *40*

Chief Comcomly, *8, 16*

Chief Joseph, *8, 112, 113*

Chimney Rock, *120*

Christmas Valley National Back Country Byway, *127, 128, 133–137*

Christmas Valley Sand Dunes, *133, 134, 136*

Clackamas River, *49, 52*

Clackamas River Trail, *52*

Clear Lake, *56, 57*

Clearwater Falls, *72*

Cloud Cap, *48*

Coast Range, *15, 17, 32*

Coffin Mountain , *56*

Colliding Waters, *72*

Colony Rock, *28*

Columbia River, *12, 40, 45*

Columbia River Gorge National Scenic Area, *40–43*

Constitution Grove, *61*

Coquille River, *76, 80*

Corps of Discovery, *16, 17*

Corvallis, *32, 33*

Cougar Reservoir, *60, 61*

Covered Bridge Country Tour, *35, 36–37*

Crack-in-the-Ground, *127, 133, 136–137*

Crater Lake, *4, 67, 68, 72–73, 81, 82, 83, 85*

Crater Lake National Park, *4, 85*

Crooked Wild and Scenic River, *119–121, 124*

Crown Point, *44*

Cultus Lake, *65*

Dalles, The, *40, 45*

Davis Lake, *65*

Dean Creek Elk Viewing Area, *32*

Dee Wright Observator, *57*

Depoe Bay, *28*

Deschutes River, *64, 94, 96*

Devils Garden Lava Flow, *65, 133*

Diamond Craters Outstanding Natural Area, *144–145*

Diamond Lake, *70, 72–73, 74*

Diamond Loop National Back Country Byway, *142*

Eagle Cap Wilderness, *109*

Elk Creek Falls, *80*

Elk Lake, *65*

Elkhorn Crest, *113*

Elkhorn Scenic Byway, *104, 116*

Fishhawk Falls, *16*

Flagstaff Hill, *113*

Florence, *29*

Fort Clatsop National Memorial, *16, 17*

Fort Hoskins Historic Park, *33*

Fort Klamath, *84–85*

Fort Rock State Park, *133*

Fossil, *101, 104*

Foster Reservoir, *53, 56*

Fremont National Forest, *128, 152, 155*

Fremont Powerhouse, *117*

Frenchglen, *144, 148, 152, 153*

Galice-Hellgate National Back Country Byway, *88–89*

Gilkey Covered Bridge, *7, 36*

Gold Beach, *68, 76–77, 78, 80*

Goose Lake, *133*

Gordon House, *25*

Grave Creek to Marial National Back Country Byway, *88–89*

Green Peak Falls, *32*

Green Peter Reservoir, *53, 56*

Haines, *116*

Hannah Covered Bridge, *37*

Harris Covered Bridge, *33*

Hart Mountain, *152, 153, 154*

Hart Mountain National Antelope Refuge, *152, 153, 154–155*

Heceta Head Lighthouse, *29*

Hells Canyon Overlook, *112*

Hells Canyon Scenic Byway, *7–8, 109–113*

Henderson Grave, *137*

Heppner, *105*

Historic Columbia River Highway, *7–8, 40–45*

Hoffman Covered Bridge, *36*

Hood River, *45, 47, 49*

Jesse Settlemier House, *21, 27*

Jewell Meadows Wildlife Area, *14, 16*

John B. Yeon State Park, *44*

John Day, *102, 104, 121, 125*

John Day Fossil Beds National Monument, *99, 101*

John Day River, *100–101*

Jordan Valley, *137, 138, 140–141*

Joseph, *92, 109, 111, 112, 113*

Journey Through Time Scenic Byway, *100–104, 116, 117*

Kam Wah Chung & Company Museum, *102, 104*

Keeney Pass, *137, 140*

Kiger Gorge Viewpoint, *149*

Kiger Mustang Management Area, *141, 145*

Kiger wild horses, *145, 149*

Klamath Basin, *68, 81, 83*

Klamath Wildlife Area, *83, 88*

Lakeview, *128, 152*

Lakeview to Steens National Back Country Byway, *152–155*

Larch Mountain, *44*

Larwood Covered Bridge, *35, 37*

Leslie Gulch–Succor Creek Backroad, *137–141*

Lewis and Clark, *8, 12, 16, 17, 48*

Lighthouses, *20, 28–29, 30, 80*

Lincoln City, *25, 28, 30*

Little Blitzen Gorge, *149, 152*

Lost Creek Reservoir, *70*

Lost Forest, *33, 136*

Lost Lake, *45–49*

Lower Crooked River National Back Country Byway, *119–121*

Lower Deschutes River National Back Country Byway, *96–97*

Lower Rogue River, *76–77*

Lower Rogue Trail, *77*

Macks Canyon Recreation Site, *97*

Malheur National Wildlife Refuge, *141, 143, 144, 148*

Malheur National Wildlife Refuge–Diamond Loop, *141–145*

Mary D. Hume, 78, 80

Marys Peak, *32*

Maupin, *94, 96*

McCullough, Conde B., *27*

McKenzie River, *57, 60, 64*

McKenzie Pass–Santiam Pass Scenic Byway, *56–60*

Metolius River, *54, 60*

Mill Creek Falls Scenic Area, *73*

Mosier Twin Tunnels, *45*

Mount Angel, *21, 24*

Mount Hood, *40, 45–49*

Mount Hood–Lost Lake Loop, *45*

Mount Mazama, *48, 67, 72, 81, 85, 136*

Multnomah Falls, *39, 44*

National Historic Oregon Trail Interpretive Center, *113*

Nehalem Highway, *16*

Nestucca River National Back Country Byway, *17–21*

Newport, *28, 29, 30–31*

Nez Perce, *92, 109, 113*

North Fork John Day Wild and Scenic River, *105, 107–108, 116, 117*

North Fork of the Middle Fork Willamette River, *58, 60–61*

North Umpqua National Recreation Trail, *72*

North Umpqua Wild and Scenic River, *72–73*

Office Bridge, *39, 61*

Olallie Lake Scenic Area, *49, 51, 52*

Oregon Dunes National Recreation Area, *29, 32*

Oregon Garden, *24–25*

Oregon Outback, *127–155*

Oregon Outback Scenic Byway, *128–133*

Oregon Trail, *12, 33, 45, 48, 53, 105, 109, 113, 137, 139, 140*

Osprey Observation Point, *65*

Owyhee Reservoir, *137, 140*

P Ranch, *141, 143, 144*

Pacific City, *20*

Pacific Coast Scenic Byway, *7–8, 25–32*

Paisley, *128*

Panorama Point, *45*

Paulina/Izee Highway, *121–125*

Philomath, *33*

Picture Rock Summit, *132*

Plush, *152*

Portland Women's Forum State Park, *44*

Post, *124*

Potamus Point, *108*

Powers, *76, 80*

Prineville, *120, 121, 124*

Prospect, *72, 73*

Proxy Falls, *57*

Quartzville Creek, *53, 56, 159*

Quartzville National Back Country Byway, *53–56*

Rainie Falls, *89*

Rand Ranger Station, *89*

Reedsport, *25, 29, 32*

Riddle Brothers Ranch National Historic District, *149, 150, 152*

Riverside National Recreation Trail, *52*

Before the advent of motor vehicles, horse-drawn wagons were used to carry freight over the mountains, as shown here in Willamette National Forest during the early 1900s. (Courtesy of the United States Forest Service)

Roaring River Fish Hatchery, *37*
Robert Aufderheide Memorial Drive, *58, 60–64*
Rogue-Coquille Scenic Byway, *67, 76–80*
Rogue River National Recreation Trail, *77, 89*
Rogue River Ranch, *77, 87, 88*
Rogue-Umpqua Scenic Byway, *70, 71, 72–76*
Rogue Wild and Scenic River, *68, 72–73, 77–78, 86–87, 88–89*
Rowena Crest Viewpoint, *45*
Scio, *35, 36*
Scott Lake, *57, 58*
Sea Lion Caves, *29*
Shaniko, *100–101, 102–103*
Shepperds Dell Falls, *44*
Sherars Falls, *96–97*
Shimanek Covered Bridge, *36–37*
Silver Falls Tour Route, *21–25, 27*
Silver Falls State Park, *24, 25, 26*

Silverton, *21, 24–25*
Siskiyou Mountains, *68, 73, 76, 79, 89*
Sisters, *56, 59*
Snake River, *92, 109, 113, 137, 140*
South Breitenbush Gorge, *53*
South Fork John Day River, *121, 125*
South Fork McKenzie River, *58, 60, 61*
Sparks Lake, *61*
Squaw Lake Lava Flow, *133, 136*
Steens Mountain, *141, 148–152*
Steens Mountain National Back Country Byway, *8, 145, 148–152*
South Fork Coquille River, *79, 80*
Succor Creek, *137, 140*
Summer Lake Wildlife Area, *128, 131, 132*
Sumpter Valley Dredge, *117*
Sumpter Valley Railroad, *117*
Sweet Home, *53*

Swick Creek Old Growth Interpretive Trail, *125*
Table Rocks, *73, 76*
Terwilliger Hot Springs, *61, 64*
Three Capes Scenic Route, *17–21*
Tillamook, *17, 18, 20–21*
Timberline Trail, *48, 49*
Ukiah, *105, 108*
Union Creek, *73*
Upper Klamath National Wildlife Refuge, *85, 88*
Upper Rogue National Recreation Trail, *73*
U-pick/we-pick farms, *11, 23, 24*
Vale, *137, 139, 140*
Vernonia, *15*
Vista House, *44*
Volcanic Legacy Scenic Byway, *7–8, 81–88*
Wahkeena Falls, *44*
Wallowa Lake, *112, 113*
Wallowa Mountains, *92, 109–113*

Warner Lakes Basin, *152–153*
Watson Falls, *72*
West Cascades Scenic Byway, *49–53*
West, Oswald, *25*
Westfir, *60–61*
Whales, *19, 20, 25, 28, 30*
Whitehorse Falls, *72*
White River State Park, *97*
Wickiup Reservoir, *65*
Wildhorse Lake, *149, 151*
Willamette Valley, *11, 12, 21, 23, 24, 40, 45*
William L. Finley National Wildlife Refuge, *32*
Willow Creek, *105*
Wineries, *33*
Winter Ridge, *132*
Woodburn, *21, 24, 27*
Yaquina Head, *28, 30*

SUGGESTED RESOURCES

Hart Mountain National Antelope Refuge: 541-947-3315.

Kam Way Chung & Company Museum: 541-575-0028 (city of John Day) or 1-800-551-6949 (state parks information line).

National Park Service tour and ticket reservation line: 1-800-967-2283. For tickets to Fort Clatsop shuttle service.

Nature of the Northwest: www.naturenw.org. Offers information on Northwest forest recreation passes.

Oregon Tourism Commission: 1-800-547-7842, www.traveloregon.com.

GEOGRAPHY
McArthur, Lewis A. *Oregon Geographical Names*, 6th ed. Portland, Ore.: Oregon Historical Society Press, 1992.

GEOLOGY
Alt, David, and Donald W. Hyndman. *Roadside Geology of Oregon*. Missoula, Mont.: Mountain Press Publishing, 2001.

HISTORY
DeVoto, Bernard, editor. *The Journals of Lewis and Clark*. Boston, Mass.: Houghton Mifflin Company, 1953.

NATURAL HISTORY
Jolley, Russ. *Wildflowers of the Columbia Gorge: A Comprehensive Field Guide*. Portland, Ore.: Oregon Historical Society Press, 1988.

Little, Elbert L. *The Audubon Society Field Guide to North American Trees (Western Region)*. New York, N.Y.: Alfred A. Knopf, 1980.

Scott, Shirley L., editor. *National Geographic Society Field Guide to the Birds of North America*. Washington, D.C.: National Geographic Society, 1996.

Spellenberg, Richard. *The Audubon Society Field Guide to North American Wildflowers*. New York, N.Y.: Alfred A. Knopf, 2001.

CAMPING
Ostertag, Rhonda, and George Ostertag. *Camping Oregon*. 1st ed. Guilford, Conn.: Globe-Pequot Press, 1999; 2d ed., Guilford, Conn.: Globe-Pequot Press, 2005.

On Quartzville Creek, the often steep banks contribute to a pristine shoreline. Graceful maples, cedars, and mossy rocks accent the scenic waterway.

ABOUT THE AUTHOR
AND PHOTOGRAPHER

For the past twenty years, Rhonda and George Ostertag have been wearing-out tires and hiking boots while uncovering Oregon's prized natural haunts. The state is well celebrated in their articles, calendars, and postcards, and is featured in a half dozen of the duo's eighteen outdoor guidebooks, including *Camping Oregon* (a Globe-Pequot FalconGuide) and *Best Short Hikes in Northwest Oregon* and *100 Hikes in Oregon* (The Mountaineers Books). They do slip away from Oregon from time to time, as seen by their other titles: *California State Parks: A Complete Recreation Guide* (The Mountaineers Books), and *Hiking New York*, *Hiking Southern New England*, *Hiking Pennsylvania*, and *Scenic Driving Pennsylvania* (all Globe-Pequot titles).